THE SUPER COOL SCIENCE OF
STAR WARS

The Saber-Swirling Science Behind the Death Star, Aliens, and Life in That Galaxy Far, Far Away!

MARK BRAKE

coauthor of *The Science of Star Wars* and
author of *The Super Cool Science of Harry Potter*

Sky Pony Press
New York

Sky Pony Press books may be purchased in bulk at special discounts for sales promotion, corporate gifts, fund-raising, or educational purposes. Special editions can also be created to specifications. For details, contact the Special Sales Department, Sky Pony Press, 307 West 36th Street, 11th Floor, New York, NY 10018 or info@skyhorsepublishing.com.

Sky Pony® is a registered trademark of Skyhorse Publishing, Inc.®, a Delaware corporation.

Visit our website at www.skyponypress.com.

10 9 8 7 6 5 4 3 2 1

Library of Congress Cataloging-in-Publication Data is available on file.

Cover design by Daniel Brount
Cover photos by gettyimages

Print ISBN: 978-1-5107-5378-5
Ebook ISBN: 978-1-5107-5379-2

Printed in China

TABLE OF CONTENTS

INTRODUCTION

I have a long history with *Star Wars* and sci-fi. In the same summer that brought *Star Wars: Episode I: The Phantom Menace*, I'd set up planet Earth's first science and science fiction university degree program. The world's press were very interested, of course. So I told them the program would allow students to study "science fiction—from Mary Shelley's *Frankenstein* to the current *Star Wars* movie." Back in 1999, the program looked at "the link between science fiction and 'real' science." And ever since I've been doing just that: Writing books that look at the link between sci-fi and the real science behind it.

This book does the same. Through the stories of *Star Wars*, we see our universe in a new light. Almost on a daily basis, science shows us something new, and even shocking, about the world in which we live. It may even make us think again about the way we relate to the rest of the universe. You know the kind of thing I mean. The countless galaxies in the cosmic deep, wheeling their way through space-time. The rise of the robot: What does the future hold for humans, as the number of robots grows? The discovery of the human genome: What will humans one day become, if we are able to engineer ourselves? The universe, it seems, is a strange place, and getting stranger all the time!

Science fiction like *Star Wars* is made as a kind of answer to the strangeness of the universe. And the stories of *Star Wars* help us come to terms with this new universe, as it is uncovered by science. *Star Wars* helps us think about the "taste," the feel, and the meaning of the new discoveries of science. *Star Wars* puts a human face back on to the universe. It makes human what was once alien.

Sure, maybe there are more stars in the universe than grains of sand on all of Earth's beaches. Perhaps 100 billion galaxies flow in deep space, outside our "tiny" Milky Way. But *Star Wars* makes you feel we could still own our galaxy. Earth may no longer sit at the center of the universe. Our sun may no longer be the only star with planets. But with small steps and an outward urge (and hopefully our own *Millennium Falcon*!), the galaxy could someday be ours.

The science of space is strange indeed. But so is the science of biology. Darwin's theory of how things evolve was a big step in our understanding of all things. But Darwin's theory doesn't just apply to planet Earth. It applies to all other planets on which life arises. And so Darwin's discovery has had a huge impact both on how we see ourselves as humans and on the idea of alien life in the universe.

Star Wars helps. Its stories help us imagine what life might be like on alien planets and in extraterrestrial settings. So there's something revolutionary about *Star Wars*. Painting pictures of the universe, as it does, has a huge effect on us—we see the cosmos has changed in our minds. By imagining the strange worlds of *Star Wars*, we come to see life in the universe in a new way.

It's so easy to be dazzled by the infinity of visions *Star Wars* shows us. All those star systems and planets, alien species and spaceships, droids and cyborgs, light tricks and life forces. But, when you think about it, *Star*

Wars is simpler. It's all about the relationship between what's human and what's not human.

So that's how this book is set out. It's divided into four themes: space travel, space, aliens, and tech. Each of these themes is a way of looking at the relationship between what's human and what's not human. Taking a closer look at these themes will show us the genius of *Star Wars*, as if a glowing lightsaber were being held to it! It will show the way in which *Star Wars* works.

Space travel. Having the vast theater of space is one thing. But how do you get from one star system to another? This theme deals with the question of journeying to the stars, including faster-than-light travel, hyperspace, and a certain space station.

Space. Space in *Star Wars* is a vast theater in which the stories unfold. But it's also a feature of the nonhuman, natural world, filled with stars and habitable planets.

Aliens. If space truly is a vast theater of planets, then what kind of creatures lurk in the depths of space? *Star Wars* has created some of the most famous alien life-forms in all of film and fiction.

Tech. What will the future bring in the form of machines? *Star Wars* has plenty to say about the rise of the robot. And what might humans one day become? Whether through redesigning our genes, or using tech, *Star Wars* takes a peek at our future.

Before we begin, here's a tip on how to get your head around the idea of the huge universe in which we live. When I was in school, for some reason lost to me now, my friends and I used to fill in the "This Book Belongs To" section in the following way:

Name: _____

Address: _____

City: _____

State: _____

Country: _____

Continent: _____

Planet: Earth _____

Star System: Sol _____

Galaxy: Milky Way _____

Galaxy Supercluster: Virgo _____

Filling in your own details may help you begin your journey from our planet Earth, and out to that galaxy far, far away. So join me now in my open-minded search for science in the world's most popular science fiction universe.

Mark Brake, 2020

PART I
SPACE TRAVEL

HOW HAS *STAR WARS* INFLUENCED THE WAY WE THINK ABOUT SPACE TRAVEL?

Science fiction like *Star Wars* is not just in the movies anymore. Why? Think about the world in which you live. For the first time in history, media headlines talk about the discovery of planets outside our solar system. Planets that may look like Tatooine and Hoth. When you switch on your television, you get glimpses of a future that will soon see cars driven by droids. Space stations orbit our planet, and robotic space probes rendezvous with asteroids. Scientists tell us that the spacecraft of the future will use solar sails, in a similar way to the solar panels used by the Empire's TIE fighters in *Star Wars*. You already live in a science fiction world, just like in the movies!

In China in 2007, they had their first ever science fiction convention. They hadn't allowed science fiction for many years. What had changed? Simple, said the Chinese. We are brilliant at making things if other people bring us the plans. But we do not invent. We do not imagine. So the Chinese sent some of their people to the United States to visit Apple, Microsoft, and Google. And they asked these companies how they went about inventing the future. This is what they found: lots of inventors and engineers and scientists had read science fiction when they were young.

And, of course, they found that *Star Wars* has inspired many people. *Star Wars* has been one of the main factors that means you live in a science fiction world.

Fact Blurs with Fiction

Just look at NASA. There was a time when they named their missions after highfalutin Greek and Roman gods: space missions had names like Apollo, Mercury, and Magellan. But NASA has now jumped boldly on the *Star Wars* bandwagon. They know that many of their scientists and engineers are inspired by *Star Wars*. So NASA has now turned to *Star Wars* to inspire future generations of astronauts. Just look at what NASA astronaut Kjell N. Lindgren has to say. Kjell was flight surgeon and engineer aboard Expedition 44/45 in July 2015, on the International Space Station:

> *Star Wars* is definitely the first movie I remember seeing. I must have been three or four at the time. I'm also just a big fan of science fiction and speculative fiction, in general. And my father was in the Air Force, and I grew up on Air Force bases. I think all those things, taken together, influenced my desire to become an astronaut. It's what I wanted to do for as long as I can remember. I think *Star Wars*, just the story, of course, captures the imagination. And then also, the technology and the idea of living in space and doing all those things is very exciting as well. I've never let go of that. It's interesting, because *Star Wars* is a cultural touchstone, and we're in a generation

of astronauts now that saw *A New Hope*, *The Empire Strikes Back*, and *Return of the Jedi* when they were little kids. *Star Wars* is one of the many reasons that I became interested in spaceflight.

Kjell Lindgren also conjured up the idea of a *Star Wars*–themed mission poster. NASA gave it their backing. The poster shows the crew kitted out as Jedi Knights, lightsabers in hand. Behind them we spy a star field, with an X-wing-type satellite. And the official name of the mission is "Space Station: Expedition XLV—The Science Continues!"

Lindgren is far from the only one. NASA booths are a frequent sight at *Star Wars* conventions. The space agency has *Star Wars* "May the Fourth" Day celebrations. NASA has a commercial crew and cargo program named C3PO (Commercial Crew & Cargo Program Office), which wishes to "extend human presence in space by enabling an expanding . . . space transportation industry." And check this out: a planet scientists call Kepler-16b has been found outside the solar system. Kepler-16b orbits two suns! And it was NASA that started calling Kepler-16b "Tatooine." NASA said "the existence of a world with a double sunset, as portrayed in the film *Star Wars* more than 30 years ago, is now scientific fact."

Star Wars and Science

The *Star Wars* stories are what we call science fiction, or sci-fi for short. Sci-fi is very old. In fact, it's as old as modern science, which first emerged around 500 years ago. Way back in those days, a scientific revolution happened. Humans began to realize that they kind of lived on an alien planet. What do we mean by this? Well, all those years ago, astronomers made the most earth-shattering discovery: we do not live at the center of the universe. Until this revolution, we thought that living on Earth meant we were at the center. But when we made the discovery that we did not, two things happened. For one, it meant that the earth was now a planet, and if the earth was a planet, then the other planets might be like Earth. Which meant they might have people living on them, what we now call aliens! And another thing: the discovery made the universe seem a much bigger and weirder place! The universe of our ancestors had been small. It had been static, which meant we used to think it didn't change much over time. And the old universe had been Earth-centered. Humans were the most important thing living in it. But the new universe wasn't about us humans. It was a huge, alien void, with maybe no meaning at all.

So, *Star Wars* stories of space travel help us make sense of the new universe. We may not be at the center anymore. But we can tell tales about where we are in space and time, stories about the rise of the robot, and tales of the Sith monster within us! *Star Wars* is a way of working out how the science of the future might look for humans.

This is how sci-fi like *Star Wars* has always worked. Storytellers and movie directors are better at showing us what new scientific discoveries mean for humans. So *Star Wars* is a special way of thinking about science. It makes stories about the new worlds uncovered by science discovery and exploration. Sci-fi uses the strange worlds of the imagination to work out what it means to be alive in this new universe. *Star Wars* has shaped the way we see and do things, the way we dreamed of things to come. It helped us discover the weirdness of space, the ordinary and the extraordinary, and forced us to explore the future we now live in.

HOW COULD SPACERS TRAVEL TO OTHER GALAXIES IN *STAR WARS*?

Sometimes, it seems like there are two universes. The first universe, our actual universe, is the one in which we live. And the other universe is the fictional universe in which all the *Star Wars* stories happen. But that galaxy, far, far away must be in our actual universe. After all, if you look up the word "universe" on Google, it will say something like: universe—"everything that exists, especially all the stars, planets, and galaxies in space."

Now, astronomers think our universe has around 2 trillion galaxies in it. Yes, that's right. There are 2,000,000,000,000 galaxies in our universe! So, if a space-farer in *Star Wars* wanted to travel to another of those galaxies, how might they do that? Let's do a thought experiment to try and work out how. We will assume that the *Star Wars* galaxy has a science similar to our own, as that's what astronomers mostly always do when they think about other places in space.

Beyond That Galaxy, Far, Far Away

According to some stories, the *Star Wars* galaxy had close companion galaxies. In terms of *Star Wars* space travel, these companions would have been quite easy to travel to. There were seven companion dwarf galaxies in orbit around the main *Star Wars* galaxy. They were named, in alphabetical order, Aurek, Besh, Cresh (I'm not making this up), Dorn, Esk, Forn, and Grek. Apart from the names, all of this is perfectly in order. For example, our Milky Way galaxy also has companion galaxies in orbit around it. About fifty of them, in fact! Of those fifty, the only companion galaxies stargazers can see with their naked eye are the Large and Small Magellanic Clouds. They've been visible since ancient times, but were named after a Portuguese explorer called Magellan who spotted them in 1519. Sadly, this kind of thing happened a lot in history, where some European goes to another part of the world and names something after himself (yes, it's almost always men who did it).

The largest of the Milky Way companion galaxies is the Sagittarius Dwarf Elliptical Galaxy. What a name we've given it! Maybe we should forgive Magellan? The Sagittarius Dwarf is 8,500 light-years across, which is around ten times smaller than the Milky Way. Curiously, given its size, Sagittarius Dwarf wasn't discovered until 1994. Why? Well, even though it's one of the closest companion galaxies to the Milky Way, it's on the opposite side of our galaxy from the earth, which makes it very difficult to spot.

Intergalactic Travel

Is there space travel to companion galaxies in any *Star Wars* stories? Yes, there is! The main *Star Wars* galaxy is home to 5–20 million different intelligent alien species. Over 100 quadrillion aliens are said to have lived in 1 billion star systems. And these peoples interacted with one another through trade, war, and, of course, travel. You can't trade with someone, and especially can't fight with them, if you don't travel to them first!

Of the companions, Aurek was also known as the Rishi Maze. This was because it had a planet called Rishi, which was the starting place for hyperspace travel into Companion Aurek. Some of the Companions were said to house some 20 billion stars. The Companions were ranked in order of distance, with Companion Besh 150,000 light-years away from the main galaxy, and only ever surveyed by pro-bots, probe droids specially designed for recon missions.

Is this similar to our Milky Way galaxy? Pretty much. Of the fifty companion galaxies of the Milky Way, around eight are within 100,000 light-years. Of those, the Ursa Major II Dwarf (Uma II) galaxy sits almost at the 100,000-light-year boundary from the Milky Way. Uma II has a mass of about 5 million suns, and is thought to have formed at least 10 billion years ago. The stars of Uma II were probably among the first to form in the entire universe!

That Good Old Hyperspace Disturbance

So *Star Wars* stories admit that at least some intergalactic travel has happened. *Star Wars* spacers could journey to the companion galaxies, but no farther. Why? Because of something called a "hyperspace disturbance" beyond the edge of the main *Star Wars* galaxy. This "disturbance" made further exploration tricky. The "disturbance" was meant to be a band of swirly space, spun around the galaxy's edge.

This made it hard to cross. And beyond the galaxy's rim was a vast expanse of starless space, known as the Intergalactic Void.

To those of you readers with a more scientific mind, all this business of a "hyperspace disturbance" might sound like a bit of an excuse. Or, if you know anything about the history of the movies, it sounds much like a MacGuffin. What's a MacGuffin? The idea of a MacGuffin was made famous by British movie director Alfred Hitchcock. A MacGuffin is a plot device like the journey in *Lord of the Rings*, or a desired object, such as the Infinity Stones in the Marvel Universe stories, or in this case a "hyperspace disturbance beyond the edge of the galaxy." It's something that drives the story onward. Or rather, in this case with *Star Wars*, it doesn't drive the story forward! The writers of some of the *Star Wars* tales may have felt that, with 1 billion star systems and 5–20 million different alien species, they already had enough to explore! Their story was already pretty much driven.

But let's think even more deeply still about these *Star Wars* galaxies. If spacers can't travel beyond the "hyperspace disturbance," then they're living in a huge island in space, aren't they? They're kind of stranded in space. Now many movies use the idea of a remote and "alien" island  as the venue for a story. An island is used in old but still famous stories such as *Robinson Crusoe* and, of course, *Jurassic Park*. It even applies to the Harry Potter stories, since the tales unfold at Hogwarts School of

Witchcraft and Wizardry—a remote "island" found beyond the real "Muggle" world of non-magic.

Beyond the Hyperspace Disturbance

There isn't a "hyperspace disturbance" in the actual universe. But there is an Intergalactic Void. Astronomers on Earth have done surveys of the night sky and mapped as much of space as they can. This map is so huge we would call it a gargantuan map (look "gargantuan" up on Google, and you'll find it means "wallopingly huge").

And what have the mapmakers learned about space? The structure of the universe begins at the level of stars, such as our sun. Stars are organized into galaxies. There's little new about that! But astronomers think there are structures larger than galaxies—groups of galaxies, clusters of galaxies, and even superclusters of galaxies! Some of these structures are so big that they form walls and filaments, as astronomers call them. The walls and filaments are many millions of light-years across. And they're sometimes separated by huge voids of a similar 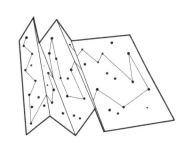 size and create a vast structure that looks like a sponge and is often called the "cosmic web"! So *Star Wars* was right. There is an intergalactic void. Though maybe it's more like an inter-filament void. And it is huge. But the void wouldn't stop spacers traveling from galaxy to galaxy, through groups and clusters, along filaments, many millions of light-years long.

HOW MUCH WOULD IT COST TO BUILD A DEATH STAR?

Just think about the sheer size of the Death Star. Death Star I was moon-sized. In our solar system, moons come in all sizes. Some of the sixty-odd moons in orbit around Jupiter are tiny, only one or two miles in diameter. Saturn's moon Titan, the biggest of the moons in the solar system, is a huge 3,200 miles across. Our moon is 2,158 miles in diameter, about a quarter the size of the earth.

The diameter of Death Star I was seventy-five miles. So, that's a moon-sized (and shaped) space station, with its own gravity, and enough living space inside for a crew of 342,953 Imperial Army and Navy personnel, and a further 25,984 stormtroopers. That's some construction!

Then you have to add the kind of creature comforts most other Imperial military postings simply didn't have: recreation areas, cantinas with state-of-the-art bartender droids, and, famously, a canteen. Then you begin to get a better idea of the scale and cost of this Death Star venture.

The Build

Let's build one. Firstly, steel. Lots of it. In fact, gargantuan amounts of the stuff. Let's assume around one tenth of Death Star I is something other than empty space. That means our build would need about 134 quadrillion tons of steel. That's 134 thousand trillion, or 134,000,000,000,000,000 tons.

That amount of steel would cost the Imperial Exchequer around $852 quadrillion ($852,000,000,000,000,000). And cost is not the only problem! Think about how long that amount of steel takes to make. At the rate planet Earth makes steel, Death Star I would use up around 800 millennia's worth. Yes, it would take us humans 800,000 years to make that much steel! That's not far short of a million years.

Death Star I was built above the inhospitable desert world of Geonosis. And this fact reminds us of another problem. As Geonosis alone is unlikely to make enough steel for our Death Star, more steel would have to be shipped in from other worlds, at great cost. Shipping into space, off any steelmaking planet, would cost around $100 million per ton.

But there's another option on the Death Star I steel build—asteroid mining. Here on planet Earth, asteroid mining is space's new frontier. A class of asteroids known as easily recoverable objects (EROs) was found by scientists in 2013. Twelve asteroids made up the first group, all of which could be mined with existing rocket science. Of 9,000 near-Earth asteroids that were searched, these twelve could all be brought into Earth-orbit quite cheaply, and by changing their speed to less than 1,100 miles per hour.

Let's take an example asteroid: 16 Psyche. It's believed to contain a small portion of precious metals, but more importantly, 1.7×10^{19} kg of nickel–iron. That's enough to supply Earth's needs for several million years. By the way, 1.7×10^{19} kg of nickel–iron is the same as 17,000,000,000,000,000 tons of the 134,000,000,000,000,000 tons needed to build Death Star I. Just another seven asteroids like 16 Psyche and we have enough metal for the build!

How can more money be saved? Well the to-and-fro shipping and building costs could be cut down by bringing the asteroids into a safe orbit close to where the Death Star is being built. This could allow for more material to be used and less to be wasted. But, compared to the total build costs, the savings would be small.

The Cost

DS-1 Orbital Battle Station, the First Death Star, was made using the slave labor of Wookiees and various other alien species. This means that during and after the build, organic life-forms would have needed air to breathe. If we assume that six-tenths of Death Star I has its own "air" created inside the Death Star, the builders would need 8.23 quintillion cubic meters of nitrogen (the main constituent of air in Earth's atmosphere) and 1.65 quintillion cubic meters of oxygen. Delivery of these important gases would set you back $3.48 septillion for the nitrogen and $263.33 quintillion for the oxygen.

The total cost of Death Star I comes to a huge $20 septillion, or $20 000,000,000,000,000,000,000,000. That's about a trillion times the current American debt. It's also the cost of 2,000 trillion missions to Mars. That's probably enough money to move the entire population of Earth to Mars, not that anyone would be able to breathe when we got there!

And this sum of $20 septillion is the cost of just a bargain-basement Death Star. We haven't yet added crew quarters, life-support systems, computer networks, Wi-Fi, power generators, five-star luxury options, air-conditioning, mega-lasers, Darth Vader's penthouse, or the canteen. Or the labor cost of actually paying the builders, assuming we are good employers and don't use slave labor! As for Death Star II, it's 100 miles across and has 560 internal levels to accommodate about 2.5 million passengers. I'm not working that out, but why don't you try, dear reader?!

Now that we've worked out how much a Death Star costs to build, you realize that it really is a waste of money to destroy it! What could have been done with the Death Star instead? Well, some eco-friendly options were also possible. Perhaps the Death Star could have been turned into a mobile science research lab. Or how about a Death Star Holiday Destination? Using slogans such as "Picnic in Paradise," and "The Canteen at the End of the Universe," the Death Star could be moved to a star system of your choosing. What better way to use the crew quarters, five-star luxury options, turbo-elevators, galactic views, and Imperial theater systems?

On the darker side of possibilities, the Death Star could have been turned into a high-security jail, to lock up the worst elements of the Imperial regime. Think less *Prisoner of Azkaban* here, and more "Prisoner of Alderaan." Another option would be off-planet banking. The rich are always squirreling their money away where no one can find it. So the Death Star could be a place where the galaxy's wealthy elite hide their cash.

But maybe the best option for a great number of people in the galaxy would be the Death Star Discovery Center. This would be a highly mobile art museum and library. It would also have a seed bank and a treasury of rare species to protect galactic biodiversity. The Discovery Center could tour the galaxy, exhibiting cultural artifacts from every planet in the galaxy.

OUR FUTURE IS IN SPACE: IS THIS THE GREATEST OF ALL *STARS WARS* MESSAGES?

A famous American sci-fi writer called Larry Niven once said, "The dinosaurs became extinct because they didn't have a space program." His idea was this: if the dinosaurs had a base on the moon or Mars, they would not have died out. (By the way, imagine dinosaurs on the moon; wouldn't that be cool?! You might even be able to spy them through your telescope. But, then again, humans never did live alongside dinosaurs, so that's lame.) A Mars or moon base would at least have given the dinosaurs more of a chance of survival. Those raptors were smart. So, just in case we humans ever find ourselves in a kind of dinosaur situation, it might be wise to take some tips from *Star Wars*.

In *Star Wars*, a space program meant that humans got out from the Core Worlds to build a Galactic Republic over many worlds. This Galactic Republic stayed in power for 25,000 years. Human civilization has been around for only 10,000 years or so, and that's just on Earth. The Galactic Republic was a collection of peoples on different planets, ruled over by a caring government. It was spread out. Distributed, as they say. So it was not in danger from a single catastrophe, such as an asteroid or an attack from a Death Star!

Clear and Present Danger

How might humans end up like dinosaurs? Well, sci-fi writers and movie directors have different ways in which they see the end of the world. When we say "the end of the world," we are not talking about the most popular cantina on Koda, or the space station in the Outer Rim Territories! Let's look at some real doomsday possibilities, as they're called, and compare them with storylines in *Star Wars*.

First up is the possibility of planet Earth being hit by a comet. Such a huge impact would give off the same energy as several million nuclear weapons exploding at the same time! And that's if the comet is small, say only a few miles across. The last known impact of a truly huge object (six miles) was the "dinosaur impact" 66 million years ago. That ruffled a few feathers (yes, we now know some dinosaurs had feathers). Impact  events of that size are rare, but Earth's long history is still riddled with them, as Earth is very old. In fact, the devastation from a cometary impact would be like the earth being zapped by the Death Star!

Smaller impacts, around the size of one or two miles across, strike the earth every half a million years or so. These are often called "threshold global catastrophes." That's because they could cause food chains to collapse, both on land and at sea, by making so much dust that plants would die. Threshold impacts could also cause mega-tsunamis or global forest fires. And it'd be no good going for the "Hollywood option" of just blowing up the oncoming comet, as they do in the movies. If you nuked a comet into smithereens of space rock, it would all just rain down to Earth, in the way the Death Star should have done on Endor.

Sunburn

Okay, if we manage to avoid dangerous comets, there's still the problem of the sun. Yes, that sun, the one in the sky. It's fine now, but astronomers think that sometime in the far future it may pose a serious problem. Just as we have limited resources here on Earth, the sun too has only a fixed amount of fuel to burn. For most of its life, the sun burns hydrogen gas. But the hydrogen will run out, and the sun will turn to helium gas for its fuel. And when stars burn helium, it comes with a health warning: the sun will grow massively in size to become what astronomers call a red giant.

In a really spooky prediction, English sci-fi writer H. G. Wells imagined a red giant sun in his famous 1895 novel *The Time Machine.* When the story's time traveler reaches the end of time, he sees a sky in which the planets are spiraling toward this red giant sun, which hangs motionless in a kind of endless sunset.

It turns out that H. G. Wells was right. If scientists have done their math right, something like this will actually happen. In the distant future, perhaps as much as 5 billion years, our sun is expected to become a red giant, expanding to 200 times its present size. When that happens, the sun is expected to swallow up the inner planets, including Earth. It seems there's more of a chance of survival on Mars, so taking the *Star Wars* message of space travel would be a good idea!

The Space Age

So the evidence is clear. To survive, we need a space program. Like the humans from the Core Worlds in *Star Wars*, we need to form a Galactic Republic. *Star Wars* is our best example of a human population in space.

We've made a start. The Space Age is now over fifty years old. The evolution of human society has gone through Stone Age, Bronze Age, and Iron Age. The industrial revolution of the nineteenth century was often known as the Machine Age. And this Space Age we now live in began in 1957 with the launch of *Sputnik*, Earth's first artificial satellite. 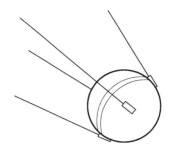 The first living creature launched into space was the dog Laika, also in 1957. Laika was followed by the first man in space, Yuri Gagarin in 1961, and the first woman, Valentina Tereshkova, in 1963. And in 1965, Alexei Leonov became the first human to walk in space.

We've learned how to live in space, too. Humans have been in orbit around the earth and learned a lot from the experience of being there. The *Mir* space station acted as a science research lab. Cosmonauts carried out experiments in biology, physics, astronomy, and meteorology. The aim of the tests was to create the new science and tech needed to live in space for longer periods. Today, the International Space Station is the result of lessons learned after many years of humans living on space stations.

The Human Future in Space

So the imaginative stories of *Star Wars* are an inspiration. But now humans need to get organized. Whether the mission is to colonize the moon or Mars, start mining in deeper space, or turn an asteroid into a space city, new ways of space living and rocket propulsion need to be worked out.

Around the time *A New Hope* was released, a group of professors met for a period of ten weeks to brainstorm the design of space colonies. What did they recommend? The building of purpose-made colonies for orbit around planets or moons. The colony would be a wheel-like habitat one mile in diameter. Space colonists would live in a tubular wheel structure, which would rotate to create gravity, and use mirrors for solar power. It's not exactly the Death Star, but it's a start!

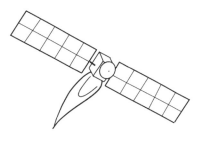

Scientists have also looked into building spacecraft propelled by nuclear power. Nuclear fuels are lighter and more efficient, and could take a craft much farther into deep space—but they are not always safe to use. Another idea would be to use an ion engine. This is where charged particles are focused into a beam. The beam creates thrust, which pushes the spacecraft in the direction of its destination.

NASA may not yet have a hyperdrive. Contrary to propaganda, the Russians are not building a Death Star. But we humans are all doing what we've done for over half a century—sending spacecraft out into the solar system and beyond, and gazing into deep space with telescopes that peer at galaxies far, far away, and dreaming of a *Star Wars* future.

WHAT WOULD IT BE LIKE, TRAVELING AT LIGHT SPEED?

Let's imagine Rey is soaring through the sky of Jakku, at night. No starship, no speeder—just Rey. Somehow. Perhaps she's salvaged some kind of repulsorlift tech, and is wearing it around her waist! She's really tearing through that night sky. In fact, she's shifting at the speed of light. Don't worry too much about how she got to that speed. This is *Star Wars*, after all. She cuts a pretty mean figure as she rips through the planet's sky, so she decides to check her reflection. She pulls a hand mirror out from her expedition backpack. She stares at the glass. She knows the light from the two moons of Jakku is enough to spy her reflection.

But what does Rey see? If she's moving at the speed of light, then the moonlight reflected from her face couldn't catch up to the mirror. That's because Rey is moving at the speed of light, and so is the mirror. This is the thing: Rey is sitting on top of the light wave, so the light from her face can't catch up to the mirror!

That's a bit weird, isn't it? Rey's image would disappear, vampire-like. (In some cultures, vampires don't have a reflection and don't cast a shadow. Maybe it's because vampires don't have a "soul.") But this isn't

Bram Stoker's *Dracula*. This is *Star Wars*. And we are doing what's known as a thought experiment on Rey.

The Experiment Continues

Rey's image on Jakku should not disappear. Whether the starlight is pure, or reflected as moonlight, Rey's image should strike the mirror. But, let's talk about the science of that image not disappearing. Imagine Finn is also on Jakku. In fact, he's on the outskirts of the Imperial Research Base, in Carbon Ridge.

Finn has picked up some of Rey's scavenging skills and he's managed to salvage some macro-binoculars. They're the field glasses we see Obi-Wan using on Geonosis. Finn's got the special-edition specs, the model for use at night. Those macro-bins are good. They allow the user to see objects far away. Some models even enabled you to see into space from the surface of a planet.

Finn spies Rey through the super-bins. He puts the two cushioned eyecups against his face, adjusts the rangefinder, and reads the data on distance and elevation. He sees Rey, moving at light speed, and he sees her reflection in the mirror. Just to be sure, Finn uses the recording function on the macro-bins, and plays back the moving images.

But this is also strange, isn't it? Finn must be seeing the light leaving Rey's face at twice its normal speed. If Rey is moving at 186,000 miles a second, and the moonlight leaves her face at 186,000 miles a second, then relative to Finn, the light should be moving at 372,000 miles per second! That can't be right.

Something's Gotta Give

The solution to this puzzle is rather simple. And it's this: the speed of light, leaving Rey's face, has to be the same for both observers, Rey and Finn. The only trouble is, the true meaning of this solution is not simple. A thought experiment like this led famous German scientist Albert Einstein to an incredible theory. Einstein said that, if everyone (including Rey and Finn) were to see the same speed for light, then all other ideas about light motion must change. In other words, we need to think again about time, length, mass, and speed. They all have to be tossed into the dustbin of history!

So Einstein said light always moves with a definite speed, to which he gave the special symbol "c." And for us that means—whether it's Rey or Finn measuring it—the speed of light will be the same. Einstein's idea has a startling result for *Star Wars*: It means there's no such thing in nature as a journey in an instant—it takes time to get from one place to another. And that's where the deeper difficulty with *Star Wars* steps in. What would happen when a spaceship approached the speed of light?

Energy and Inertia, $E = mc^2$

When a spaceship picks up speed, it accelerates. And this acceleration grows steadily with the force applied. That means the bigger the force, the faster the ship picks up speed. But, the bigger the mass of the spaceship, the harder it is to get it moving faster. This is because the mass of any object, including spaceships, has a quality known as inertia. Inertia is

the quality that mass has by which it stays in its existing state. For example, if a ship is hurtling through space, inertia keeps it going, forever, unless some other force stops it.

Inertia is also why it's easier to get the Naboo Royal Starship rolling than it is a Trade Federation battleship. Now, Einstein said that as you give an object, such as a starship, more and more energy, rather than going faster, the starship just gets more and more massive. Think of the *Millennium Falcon*: to speed along, it needs energy. And to travel at the speed of light, the amount of energy it needs to propel it might grow to infinity! In short, to move the *Millennium Falcon* at light speed might take all of the energy in the universe. Just a small snag! No wonder the *Star Wars* writers thought they needed to invent the hyperdrive.

PART II
SPACE

WOULD THE DEATH OF THE DEATH STAR SPELL THE END OF ENDOR?

Picture the scene. Luke pilots an Imperial shuttle out of the main docking bay of the Death Star. The entire section of bay is blown away. Lando now expertly rockets the *Falcon* out of the exploding superstructure and speeds toward Endor. Just seconds later, we see the Death Star supernova into oblivion. Lando has clutched victory from the jaws of defeat.

Lando laughs. He just made it. We cut to the Endor forest, where Han, Leia, Chewie, and the Ewoks gaze up at the sky to see the Death Star's final flash of destruction. Little more than a pretty firework in the sky. Everyone cheers. Soon enough, the movie's end credits roll over a star field.

Are there science problems with this ending? Yep. First up we have to say that this scene from *Return of the Jedi* is beautifully done. Credit where credit's due. But let's take a step back and think about the science of the sequence. What would really have happened to the Ewoks on that forest moon when the second Death Star was destroyed? Would the satellite world of Endor really prove to be a sanctuary? And can the science help us imagine another ending to the movie?

The Death Star as a Moon of Endor

Let's rewrite the scene. We'll need to think about the science and get answers to some technical questions. Questions like: How big are Endor and the Death Star? How far apart do they sit in space? With how much energy will the Death Star explode, and in what way will it really explode? And how will that explosion make itself felt on the surface of the Sanctuary Moon? All pretty simple. Not.

And sure enough, from the get-go, there are problems. How big exactly is Death Star II? For this calculation, we are going to work in kilometers. Some say Death Star II is 160 kilometers, which we assume to be its diameter, as the first Death Star had a diameter of 120 kilometers. Others say that Death Star II was about 3 percent the size of Endor, which has a diameter of 4,900 kilometers. That would make the second Death Star's diameter a mere 147 kilometers.

Yet others say Death Star II had a whopping diameter of 343 kilometers! This figure of 343 kilometers is worked out by studying the actual *Star Wars* movie footage. If you measure the hologram from the pre-attack briefing scene from *Return of the Jedi*, the relative sizes of Endor and the Death Star can be calculated. Using this method, it's been worked out that, yes, Endor is 4,900 kilometers across. But the "pixelated" image of the Death Star II is not 3 percent but 7 percent of the diameter of the Sanctuary Moon. This is what gives the figure of 343 kilometers. Far from perfect, but let's go with this calculation, as it is done directly from the movie.

Death Star Sitting Pretty

Now we've worked out the sizes of the two bodies, how far apart do they sit? Knowing this will tell us how far Endor is from the blast zone. Then we can work out how much damage it might take. Gazing again at that hologram from *Return of the Jedi*, it looks like the very centers of Endor and the Death Star are about 2,910 kilometers apart. This means that the Death Star must sit at a height of 460 kilometers above the surface of Endor. Let's hope that Sanctuary Moon can take a punch or two when Death Star II explodes!

So let's look at Death Star II. It's sitting pretty up there, in the Endorian sky. How's it doing that exactly? Remember that an energy shield—coming up from the surface of Endor—protected Death Star II from attack. The shield had to be switched off before any assault on the space station could be done. To stay in touch with the shield generator, Death Star II needed to sit in the same spot above Endor. This much is clear in the pre-attack briefing scene. The kind of orbit in which Death Star II sits is known as a synchronous orbit, and it's similar to that of communication satellites around the earth.

So let's assume Death Star II is able to hang in orbit through the use of the same repulsorlift antigravity tech that's used on speeders, pod racers, and Senate pods. The Death Star II repulsorlifts would be massive, of course, as this is some job they'd be doing, keeping that huge space station in the air!

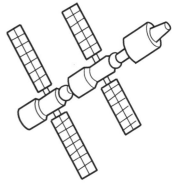

The Death Star Explodes

How would Death Star II explode? Into what kind of smithereens would it be smashed on explosion? And what would happen to those smithereens?

In the *Return of the Jedi* movie, the Death Star II explosion was little more than a pretty firework in the sky. Also, when you come to think about it, that blast is a little lame when you compare it to the detonation of the first Death Star. Death Star I seemed to go nuclear immediately on being hit by two tiny proton torpedoes. But the explosion of the second Death Star allowed rebel pilots to escape before letting loose.

The real science of what would happen is bad news for the Ewoks. That's because a real explosion won't look like a firework. It'll be a huge Death Star in smithereen supernova! Once that Death Star II is detonated, the smithereens will rain down destruction from above. The entire mass of Death Star II will just fall onto Endor. And a lot of the fallout will hit the shield generator, exactly where we find our heroes and a group of Ewoks.

But how much mass of burning Death Star II will there be? Assuming Death Star II is a similar shell-build as Death Star I, and remembering its diameter of 343 kilometers, its mass will be about 1019 kilograms. That's an interesting number. It's roughly the same as the mass of Saturn's rings—those countless smithereens, tiny and titanic, that make up the bling of the gas giant's famous halo.

So this is going to be one huge impact. The mass of smithereens would hit the Sanctuary Moon at a speed of more than 6,000 mph. The impact would make a crater 700 kilometers (435 miles) wide. That's four times bigger than the one left behind by the comet that killed the dinosaurs. And Endor is much smaller than Earth.

You can only imagine the extent of the damage. Everything on the surface of Endor would be destroyed. The moon's atmosphere would also suffer. It would be boiled by the exploding particles, tearing a path from the blast to the crater. The seas of Endor would flash into steam, as the forests began their long burn into a global firestorm that lasts way into the night. Blowing up Death Star II wasn't such a good idea!

The Death of the Death Star II, Take Two

So, let's reimagine the end sequences of the Battle of Endor: We cut to the deep forest where Han, Leia, Chewie, and the Ewoks gaze up at the supernova detonation of Death Star II. An expanding ball of fire hits the Endorian atmosphere. It's as though every star in the heavens has been hurled from its seat, and sent lawless through the wilds of the sky. As thick as scorching snowflakes, thousands of burning meteors are shooting down in every direction, with long trains of light following their course. Every heart is filled with horror at this majestic display of destruction.

Our heroes make their move. Mounting 74-Z speeder bikes, they speed through the forest as the planet burns. Keeping just ahead of the line of fiery flames, they feel the heat of the forest fires growing as they make their way to the sanctuary of the *Millennium Falcon*, where Lando waits. Mission abort. The dark side has won. For now. End credits roll over a star field.

WHAT DOES *STAR WARS* TELL US ABOUT OUR OWN MILKY WAY GALAXY?

The *Star Wars* galaxy is full of aliens. They include Arkanians, Blood Carvers and Bouncers, Crokes and Ewoks, Gungans and Hutts, Tusken Raiders, Wookiees, and Womp Rats. Altogether over 100 quadrillion aliens are said to have lived in 1 billion star systems. And, for us in our book, the geography of the *Star Wars* galaxy also gives us an interesting way to think about our own galaxy, the Milky Way.

Galaxies

Let's talk a little more about galaxies. Firstly, remember there are more stars in our universe than there are grains of sand on all of the beaches on planet Earth. It's worth pausing for a while to imagine being on one of those beaches. Soft golden sand, sweeping off into the distance. Bright sunny day, of course. In fact, let's make it the Caribbean. No expense spared. You reach down, hands cupped, and gather up two handfuls of the golden sand. Then you let the sand fall through your fingers. The grains glisten as they fall and catch the sunlight. Each grain is a star. And each star is like our own local star, the sun. You saunter on a few more steps, and again you gather up the sand and let it fall. And so on, over all the beaches on Earth. So much sand, so many stars.

A group of researchers at the University of Hawaii actually tried putting a number to the grains of sand on the world's beaches. The earth has roughly (and we're speaking very roughly here) 7.5×10^{18} grains of sand, or 7 quintillion, 500 quadrillion grains.

And yet, there are ten stars for every one of these sand grains. That's also eleven times the number of cups of water in all the earth's oceans, and 100 billion times the number of letters in the 14 million books in the Library of Congress. (These incredible stats make you think. But also remember: the number of stars in the universe is the same as the number of H_2O molecules in just ten drops of water!)

On a large scale, swarms of such stars dwell in galaxies. And these galaxies effortlessly wheel their way through the vastness of deep space. Each galaxy contains millions, if not billions, of stars. Under cover of the night sky, some galaxies can be seen with the naked eye. It's worth remembering that the very word "galaxy" comes from the Greek term *galaxias*, or "milky circle," for its appearance to the eye.

Imagine yourself again, on our same trip, under the starry reach of the Caribbean sky at night. You look up, and the star field is dazzling. But here and there is the odd fuzzy smudge of a galaxy. The great galaxy in the constellation Andromeda, for example, is one of our near neighbors, and yet even this nearby swarm of stars can only be seen in detail by telescope. So that's how galaxies look to the naked eye. Like tiny thumbprints in the sky. Yet our Milky Way galaxy holds 200–400 billion stars, and is special to us as it is the home galaxy of planet Earth.

Looking Down on a Galaxy from Above

Now imagine taking a galactic trip in the *Millennium Falcon*. Given its reputation on the Kessel Run hyperspace route, the outer reaches of our Milky Way will be like a walk in the park. The hyperdrive of the *Millennium Falcon* is engaged, and the local star-scape blurs as we fly off to the outer limits of our galaxy.

Once in position, through the window of the *Millennium Falcon*, the Milky Way is a fabulous, jaw-dropping sight. Looking down on our galaxy from above, it looks like a huge, luminous spiral, consisting of around 200 billion stars, one of which is our sun.

From one edge to the other, the Milky Way may be as much as 150,000 light-years across. We don't know for sure, as it's hard to tell how big something is when you're living inside it! Space must be truly huge, though, to house so many stars. So huge, in fact, that we need this special unit of light-years with which to measure it. A light-year is the distance light travels in 365 Earth days. Light is the fastest thing known to us. A beam of light will travel a little over 186,000 miles in one second. This means light can travel 5,874,601,670,040 miles in a year. And that also means that our Milky Way is 881,793,805,977,541,248 miles across!

The Geography of the *Star Wars* Galaxy

According to the stories, the *Star Wars* galaxy is around the same size as our own. It's divided into regions, with the Deep Core as the central and brightest region of its space. The populous Core Worlds are where the human species first evolved. The Core includes planets such as Alderaan and Coruscant, which were granted permission to settle new planets. They were followed by the Colonies (which included the planets Castell and Halcyon), the Inner Rim (which housed the world of Onderon), the Expansion Region (housing the likes of Aquaris), and the Mid Rim (which included Naboo), and Outer Rim Territories (which included Hoth and Tatooine).

The areas of the *Star Wars* galaxy were sometimes known as the galactic north, south, east, and west. The Unknown Regions existed to the galactic west. They were mostly unexplored as the many trade routes headed in the direction of the galactic east. Wild Space referred to regions at the very edge of the galaxy. They were inhabited by intelligent species, but never fully explored and mapped.

Almost all of the inhabited worlds—Tatooine, Naboo, Hoth, and so on—lie in the Expansion Region of the galaxy. Looking down from above, the Expansion Region would sit on the right of our stunning sight. Jakku, Endor, and Coruscant sit around the galactic core. If this layout of worlds were the same in our galaxy, then our sun and its family of planets could be sitting in the Milky Way's version of the Unknown Regions. It might even be called the dark side of the galaxy!

The Fermi Paradox

In fact, the *Star Wars* galaxy might tell us something about the possibility of life beyond the earth in our Milky Way. For centuries humans have wondered about an important question: If the galaxy is full of life, why haven't we met any aliens? This question is sometimes called the Fermi Paradox. Enrico Fermi was an Italian physicist, and he put the question like this—"Where is everybody?"

Fermi said this while he was chatting over lunch one day. The chat with his colleagues was all about whether our galaxy, like the one in *Star Wars*, has many planets with civilized people on them. Most of Fermi's colleagues thought that we humans probably have a lot of company up there in deep space. But Fermi said that if this were true, if there really are a lot of alien civilizations, then some of them would have spread out, like in *Star Wars*, and we humans would have met them by now.

Fermi's idea was a kind of *Star Wars* one. He thought that civilizations that had space travel would quickly colonize the entire galaxy. Fermi did the math: within 10 million years, every star system would meet some kind of alien visitor from afar. Now, 10 million years may sound like a long time. But it's a blink of the eye, compared with the age of a galaxy. So, Fermi said, if alien civilizations have had more than enough time to spread out into our galaxy, where are they all? Where are the legions of sleek spaceships tearing across the sky? Where are the hordes of invading aliens? Where's the future promised in sci-fi like *Star Wars*?

Solutions to the Fermi Paradox

Many people have thought about Fermi's paradox. And they've come up with some clever answers. Perhaps the aliens on some planet all argued and wiped each other out before they could invent space travel? Or maybe the stars are so far apart that space travel is simply too tricky and expensive? Maybe aliens do visit, but keep their visits secret until humans have become more grown-up and have stopped arguing with each other!

But *Star Wars* gives us another possible answer. What if the sun and the earth lie on the dark side of the galaxy? That means we are in the Milky Way's version of the Unknown Regions. So our solar system is just too far from the fashionable Core Worlds of the Milky Way. It would take a journey of trillions of miles to get to the solar system. Maybe in the Milky Way, too, there are many trade routes headed in the direction of the galactic east. But the galactic west is not yet fully explored and charted. Maybe we are not alone after all.

DID *STAR WARS* PREDICT THE EXISTENCE OF EXOPLANETS?

Remember that scene in *The Force Awakens* where Han, Rey, and Finn journey into Maz Kanata's colorful dive bar in that castle on Takodana? The bar is a haunt of freight pilots and dangerous alien pirates. And the scene reminds us of Tattooine's Mos Eisley cantina in *A New Hope*. That bar was also a dimly lit tavern, known for its strong liquor, jazzy tunes, and occasional outbreaks of fighting! And, of course, it's where Luke first meets Han. But, in these bars, where do all those alien races actually come from? The answer? Exoplanets. The planets of stars outside the solar system. Millions of them.

And those memorable scenes in the two taverns shows that, even in a playful way, *Star Wars* is doing some serious science. Why? Because it's not only showing a universe full of aliens, it's also telling us the cosmos is full of alien worlds.

The Earth Is Just a Planet

The *Star Wars* universe is a good example of the idea that our planet Earth is a planet like many others out there in deep space. Since there's life on Earth, there should also be life on earthlike planets in the universe. And that means there's nothing special about our solar system, nothing special about planet Earth's history, and nothing special about the evolution of life here. As the famous British scientist Stephen Hawking once said, "The human race is just a chemical scum on a moderate-sized planet, orbiting around a very average star in the outer suburb of one among a hundred billion galaxies."

When you think about all this, you can see why simple *Star Wars* stories are actually doing science. The stories assume a galaxy full of aliens, who have evolved on planets similar to Earth, but whose powers and tech just happen to be more advanced than ours. *Star Wars* says nothing at all about the idea that humans are somehow special or superior.

The idea that there are many inhabited planets beyond our own goes all the way back to the ancient Greeks, about 2,500 years ago. They too believed in a cosmos full of life-bearing worlds out in the depths of space. But no evidence was ever found, as they had no telescopes. Even when telescopes were invented in the early 1600s, the truth still lay beyond our senses. It slowly became clear that the stars lay at huge distances. Instead, storytellers used ideas to imagine what worlds, and what kind of creatures, existed beyond the range of our telescopes.

By 1977, when the *Star Wars* saga started, science fiction had been imagining alien worlds for around 400 years. Sci-fi had inspired real sci-ence. After many decades of stories about aliens, scientists began the search for alien intelligence in the 1960s. This was the world into which *Star Wars* was born.

Like many good sci-fi tales about space, *A New Hope* dreamed up other worlds. The desert planet of Tatooine. The mining planet of Kessel.

The gas planet of Yavin and its forest moon of Yavin 4. The rural planet of Dantooine. And the industrial planet of Corellia, Han's home world. To date, there are over fifty various exoplanets in *Star Wars*, including the latest additions, such as the ocean planet of Ahch-To and the desert planet of Jakku.

But it was only after *Star Wars* began that actual exoplanets were first discovered. In the year of *A New Hope*, NASA had launched the two robotic Voyager probes to the outer solar system. They have since become the first human-made object to enter interstellar space, traveling "farther than anyone, or anything, in history." On their journey to the stars, the Voyager probes found that the gas giant moons of Jupiter's Europa and Saturn's Titan were worlds in their own right. Scientists got excited. The asked once more: What other worlds lie beyond our system? What exoplanets are out in deepest space?

Worlds Beyond Our Sun

Today, we live in a great age of discovery for exoplanets. We live at a time about which many writers and storytellers have only dreamed. The first actual exoplanet was discovered in 1995, almost twenty years after *A New Hope*. This giant planet was found in a four-day orbit around the nearby star 51 Pegasi.

Since 1995, astronomers have been hunting for earthlike planets that orbit sun-like stars. They think there may be tens of billions of exoplanets in our galaxy alone.

A European team of scientists said that there may be billions of "super-Earth" planets in the Milky Way, which orbit at a distance that would allow water to flow freely on their surface.

The American space observatory Kepler was launched in 2009 to find earthlike planets orbiting other stars. Based on Kepler's early findings, Seth Shostak, senior astronomer at the SETI Institute, said that "within a thousand light-years of Earth," there are "at least thirty thousand habitable planets." And based on the same findings, the Kepler team think that there are "at least fifty billion planets in the Milky Way." Of those "at least five hundred million" may have life. Finally, NASA's Jet Propulsion Laboratory (JPL) said they expected there to be 2 billion "Earth analogues" in our galaxy—that is, planets very much like Earth. And what's more, there are billions of other galaxies!

A World of Your Own

Ten years before *A New Hope*, famous British science fiction writer Arthur C. Clarke had written about the possibility of other worlds beyond our solar system. "Almost certainly," he said, "there is enough land in the sky to give every member of the human species, back to the first ape-man, his own private, world-sized heaven—or hell. How many of those potential heavens and hells are now inhabited, and by what manner of creatures, we have no way of guessing."

Star Wars has helped us guess. The stories have helped us realize that the barriers of distance are crumbling as we continue to venture farther into space. *Star Wars* was not the first to imagine alien worlds. But it has conjured up a fantastic picture of what an inhabited galaxy might look like. The truth, as always, will be far stranger.

WHAT DO *STAR WARS* EXOMOONS MEAN FOR LIFE IN OUR GALAXY?

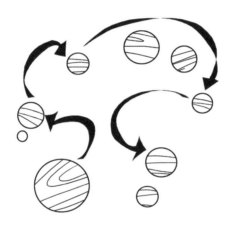

In *The Force Awakens*, we find that the planet Jakku has two exomoons. (Remember: an exoplanet like Jakku is a planet orbiting a star outside our solar system. So an exomoon is a moon that orbits an exoplanet!) And that's exactly what we have in *The Force Awakens*. Jakku and its exomoons are all orbiting a single sun.

The moons of Naboo were also habitable, and at one time had famous spice mines. But the most famous exomoon in the *Star Wars* stories has to be Endor. It's certainly been the most important in the stories. The Battle of Endor was the place of the revolution that restored the Republic. It was here that the Imperial forces kept their shield generator, which had first stopped the Alliance from destroying Death Star II.

Endor, of course, was a forest moon. It was about 3,000 miles across, which is easily bigger than our own moon. Endor was also roughly 43,000 light-years from its galaxy's center, covered in dense woodlands, and had a breathable atmosphere. Endor had two suns, Endor I and Endor II. (Some of the *Star Wars* storytellers don't seem to have had much of an imagination when it came to naming things!)

So the moons of Jakku, Naboo, and Endor are part of a growing number of *Star Wars* exomoons. Have we found anything similar in our own exploration of space? And, if so, what does it mean for life in space?

Rey the Stargazer

Let's imagine Rey as a stargazer. As a scavenger left behind on Jakku when she was a child, she had plenty of time to gaze at the stars at night. Now, the view of her night sky wouldn't be much like ours. True, she can see two moons, rather than our one. And living in the Western Reaches of the Inner Rim, her planet is closer to the core of its galaxy than Earth is to the Milky Way's. So there would have been thousands of stars visible to her naked eye, and billions beyond her sight. But, outside of the Jakku system, none of the other planets and moons of the *Star Wars* galaxy can be seen by Rey.

That's because exoplanets are very faint points of light, compared to their suns. In fact, they're usually a million times fainter than their parent stars. And exomoons would be even fainter. Rey has no chance of seeing them. Looking for them would be like looking for a needle in a haystack (assuming they have haystacks on Jakku). But the scientists of the Core Worlds would surely have known about the many exoplanets and exomoons in her galaxy. So how would they have first spotted them?

Planet Hunting with the Ancient Coruscanti

Imagine astronomers doing some planet hunting, long ago on ancient Coruscant. Their home world of Coruscant will later become the center of life in the *Star Wars* galaxy. But first, astronomers have to actually find other planets. Planet hunting is not simple stargazing. These ancient Coruscanti would have to follow the movement of neighboring stars as the stars made their way through their neighborhood of the galaxy. Some of these stars may have been seen to wobble a little.

Although the stars are huge, they're not as still as they seem in the night sky. A star like Alderaan with a satellite planet (also called Alderaan!) will move in its own wobbly orbit, due to the planet's gravity. So when the Coruscanti planet-hunters see a wobbly star, they know there may be a planet orbiting it. And, by measuring the size of the wobble, the Coruscanti can guess how big the planet might be.

In the early days, looking for wobbly stars may have been the best way for the ancient Coruscanti to find exoplanets. At least, that's how it's done here on Earth at the moment. Thousands have been found in our neighborhood of the galaxy. Planet hunters look for wobbly stars out to about 160 light-years from Earth. And, like all stars with planets, our sun wobbles too. The combined gravity of the planets in our solar system is what causes the sun's wobble. This is very true of mighty Jupiter, which is bigger than all the other planets put together.

The "Jupiter effect" will happen elsewhere in the universe, too. It doesn't have to be Jupiter itself, of course. But the Coruscanti may find a very large planet in orbit around a wobbling star. And, because bigger planets mean bigger wobbles, this way of planet hunting is best for finding other

Jupiter-like giants such as Bespin, which is about 85 percent of Jupiter's diameter.

Perhaps the Coruscanti called it the "Bespin effect"! On second thought, that's not very likely, as the Bespin system sits in Outer Rim territories and is probably impossible to "see" from Coruscant, which sits at the opposite side of the galaxy's core. They probably didn't use the wobble method for finding Alderaan either. Alderaan is a rocky planet like Earth. So it's not big enough to make a big wobble in its parent star. For smaller planets like Earth and Alderaan, you need another method: eclipses!

Coruscanti planet hunters could also have used eclipses to find exoplanets. In space, an eclipse happens when one body passes into the shadow of another. So, an eclipse of our sun happens when it moves into the shadow of our moon, and the sun cannot be seen in the usual way from Earth. In other star systems, a planet might cross in front of the parent star, causing a mini eclipse. If this happens, hunters might find an exoplanet in that system—and where there are planets, there are also moons.

The Goldilocks Zone and the Red Dwarf

The ancient Coruscanti would also be interested in Goldilocks Zones. Around a star, a planet must lie in something called the "habitable zone" to support life. The "habitable zone" is the distance around a star within which rocky planets can have liquid water on their surfaces. If a planet is beyond the habitable zone, it will not get enough of the sun's energy, and water will freeze. If a planet is closer than the habitable zone, it will get too much solar energy, and surface water will boil away. This not-too-hot, not-too-cold idea of the habitable zone is why scientists often call it the Goldilocks Zone.

So, looking for life isn't just a matter of looking for exoplanets. The Coruscanti would also have been looking for planets in Goldilocks Zones. And here, red dwarf stars become important in the hunt for exomoons. Take our Milky Way galaxy. It contains between 200 billion and 400 billion stars (the actual number may be as high as one trillion!). Around the orbits of these stars exist at least 100 billion

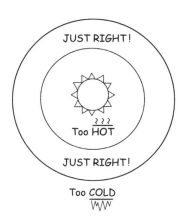

planets, many of them earthlike. Now red dwarfs might make up around three-quarters of the stars in the Milky Way. They are by far the most common type of star. The same can also be assumed of the *Star Wars* galaxy. But that provides an interesting problem for life on planets in orbit about red dwarfs.

A red dwarf is a small, cool star. Such stars have masses less than half of the sun's. At one time, astronomers thought red dwarf stars would not have habitable planets. But scientists now think that old theory is wrong. Red dwarfs do have planets. And they have interesting stories to tell. Planets in the Goldilocks Zone of a red dwarf would be so close to the parent star that they would be locked by gravity. Just like the moon in orbit about the earth, the red dwarf's planets always show the same face to their sun.

So, red-dwarf worlds are locked by the parent star's gravity. One half of the planet is always in darkness, the other half always bathed in light. They are strange and exotic worlds. On the dark side, there is a vast frozen waste. On the light side, oceans, a temperate climate, and land. But there is also a "twilight zone," an in-between place. Here in the twilight zone, between the half-worlds, strange creatures may compete for food and light. If there are any creatures at all, in such an alien world. How cool is that?!

But even if a red dwarf exoplanet is simply too weird for life, its exomoon may not be. Imagine an Earth-sized moon, in orbit around a Jupiter-sized giant. The giant may be locked in its orbit around the red dwarf. And the giant may have extreme climates on each half-world. But the exomoon in orbit around the giant may have life. Why? Because the exomoon would have a day and night cycle, as it orbited the giant. And that would mean the climate would be better for life.

Many Endors?

This is why exomoons may be so important. Since there are so many red dwarf stars in our galaxy, there will also be many exoplanets and exomoons in orbit around them. In fact, as red dwarfs make up three-quarters of the stars in the Milky Way, their exoplanets and exomoons may even be the most common type of world. And, as the exoplanets may be too weird for life, their moons may be a common home of life in the galaxy.

What's more, think about the lifetimes of red dwarf stars. They are huge. A red dwarf star with a mass about half the mass of the sun has a lifetime of 56 billion years! So, if life gets a grip on a red dwarf exomoon, the civilizations there could last for billions of years.

Could Endor be the greatest of all *Star Wars* ideas? Endor is a habitable forest moon in orbit around a hostile gas giant. The diameter of Endor is about 40 percent of the Earth's. How common are such worlds in our Milky Way?

Maybe tomorrow, or maybe a decade or century from now, we may make the most incredible discovery of all time: We may come into contact with an alien civilization. As the twenty-first century dawned, we had been imagining alien life for almost 2,500 years. Thanks to *Star Wars*, we can only wonder if that civilization lives on an exomoon like Endor.

COULD STARKILLER BASE SUCK THE ENERGY FROM A STAR, AS IN *THE FORCE AWAKENS*?

Starkiller Base. Function: Headquarters of the First Order. History: built after the blasting of the Death Star II in the skies above Endor. Technical brief: a transformed ice planet from the Unknown Regions. Starkiller Base was more than twice the size of previous battle stations, and much more powerful. (Hint: think of it as Pluto with a planet-sized pistol. In short: "Death Star III.")

Now some of you may still have some doubts about the power of this later model of a killer space station. After all, the rebels dealt easily with the first two. So, just in case, the base was shown to prove its power early on in *The Force Awakens*. It annihilated five planets at once. And, as the name Starkiller suggests, the base was powered by sucking the energy out from burning stars. But in all seriousness for the science: How might Starkiller Base have done that? And how would it have stored the energy once a star had been drained?

Atom-Smashing Machines in the Sky

Firstly, Starkiller Base is not the only atom-smashing machine. The universe is full of them. They're better known as stars. Stars power our galaxy, as they would the *Star Wars* galaxy. Stars are bringers of energy and light, the building blocks from which the entire cosmos was created. Without our own star there'd be no light, no life, no Earth as we know it.

Stars such as our sun are huge balls of burning gas. It's mostly hydrogen, but about a quarter of it is helium. Their makeup depends on how old they are. Older stars will have a greater amount of gases heavier than hydrogen and helium.

The architects of Starkiller Base would have been well aware that stars like the sun have temperatures at their centers of around 16 million degrees. That's hot enough for nuclear reactions, like turning hydrogen into helium. Atom-smashing happens in all stars, due to these huge temperatures and pressures at their very centers. To be clear, it's more like atom-fusing than atom-smashing, but the gases have to be smashed together before they can fuse.

Starkiller Base as an Atom-Smasher

Atom-smashing gives out huge amounts of energy. This energy could be sucked up by the Starkiller Base. For example, stars like our sun burn about 7 million tons of gas every second. That's as much energy as 7 trillion nuclear explosions per second. Yes, that's right: When you bask in the sun, you're basking in the glow of 7 trillion nuclear explosions a second! It's certainly enough energy to kill one planet or five.

In fact, let's use Einstein's famous equation $E=mc^2$ to work out how much energy you could get from fusing all the sun's hydrogen into helium. Plugging in the figures for the mass of the sun (that's the "m" in Einstein's equation) and the speed of light (the "c"), we get an answer of 870 million trillion trillion trillion joules of energy. That's gargantuan! Draining just the sun would make enough energy to zap 4 trillion planets, every planet in the *Star Wars* galaxy!

The Starkiller architects would have known stars are great sources of energy. And stars of the sun's mass will burn hydrogen for about 10 billion years. There is a huge range of star sizes and masses. In fact, stars of smaller mass than our sun hang around even longer. Small stars have what are called "forever lifetimes." A star half the size of our sun will go on burning for 50 billion years!

How Starkiller Base Worked and Died!

So stars are huge sources of energy. That's well-known. But how could Starkiller Base have tapped that energy to charge its big gun? According to the stories, the Starkiller Base worked by focusing on a single star as a power source. Then it would drain star stuff to power its weapon. We have already seen that there's enough energy in the sun alone to atom-smash those five planets in *The Force Awakens*.

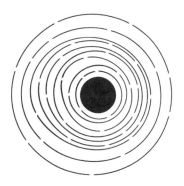

When Starkiller was working, it looked like a black hole—a vortex of heat and light, falling down into oblivion. As the Base charged up from star power, it gradually blocked out starlight until, running at full facility, it drained the star completely, leaving the surface in darkness.

And yet, as with the earlier Death Stars, the Starkiller Base had a weakness. It was destroyed by aiming at a weak point in an attack led by Poe Dameron, awesome pilot and spearhead of the Resistance. The strike made the entire Starkiller Base planet implode, thirty seconds before the superweapon fired upon the Resistance base on D'Qar. The stories say that "as it was destroyed, the stored material from the sun it drained expanded to create a new star in the planet's place, turning the star system into a binary."

WHICH EXOPLANETS ARE LIKE *STAR WARS* WORLDS?

Jakku. Tatooine. Hoth. Planet names familiar to fans of that galaxy far, far away. But what about exoplanets like Kepler-16b, 51 Pegasi b, or even OGLE-2005-BLG-390Lb? They're the given names of exoplanets found orbiting other stars in our Milky Way galaxy.

In this exoplanet battle of names between fiction and fact, the fiction of *Star Wars* got there first. It helped us conjure up a picture of what inhabited planets might look and sound like. But now astronomers are finding that our own neighborhood in space is filled with exoplanets. Many of them are as exotic as anything in *Star Wars*. And some are even spookily like their fictional cousins!

Making Sense of the Milky Way

Okay, so we are going to go on a magical mystery tour through the weird and wonderful world of exoplanets. Let's start the journey in our own backyard. After all, we can use our own solar system as a measure to size up other star and planet systems.

In our solar system, there are two kinds of planets: rocky and gassy. The basic difference is this: On rocky planets, there's somewhere to land the *Millennium Falcon*—the ground. But gassy planets don't have "grounds";

they just have gas. This makes landing more difficult! Rocky planets form close to the sun, somewhere near the Goldilocks Zone. The bigger gassy planets form farther out, beyond the frost line, and way into the cold zone.

Gassy giants have been found in other systems, too. As planet-hunters scanned the skies for wobbling stars, they already knew that bigger planets would mean bigger wobbles. And massive giants would make even bigger and faster wobbles in their parent star, making the giant easier to detect.

That's why many of the early exoplanets found were called "hot Jupiters," or maybe we could use a *Star Wars* version of "boiling Bespins"! These hot Jupiters are named this way because their mass is of Jupiter size. But their orbit is much closer to their parent star than Jupiter's is to the sun. Between 10 and 300 times closer, in fact. And that makes them hot! Being so close to the mother star means that hot Jupiters get their gassy atmospheres stripped away by the heat. So this class of exoplanet is quite unlike the livable worlds in *Star Wars*. And yet, as detection methods got better, astronomers started to find exoplanets far more in the *Star Wars* style.

Consider Kepler-16b

For example, let's talk about NASA's Kepler Mission. It was launched in 2009, and the job of the Kepler spacecraft was to spot earthlike planets among the 155,000 stars in the constellations of Cygnus and Lyra, which are visible from Earth's northern hemisphere.

Kepler was the most exciting exoplanet mission to date. The Kepler space observatory looked for earthlike planets orbiting sun-like stars. Kepler scanned the sky, looking for mini eclipses, those telltale signs that an exoplanet is crossing in front of its parent star. By using Cygnus and

Lyra as examples, the Kepler Mission also aimed to find out how many of the billions of stars in our galaxy may have earthlike worlds.

What Kepler found is quite incredible. When the observatory completed its primary mission objectives in 2012, it had found nearly 5,000 exoplanets. Perhaps its strangest discovery is a so-called Styrofoam planet, a world with just one-tenth the density of Jupiter. But its most stunning discovery is the first evidence of a rocky planet outside our solar system. In 2015, Kepler astronomers announced the discovery of the earth's "closest twin."

Kepler had also found a Tatooine-like planet in Kepler-16b. Like Tatooine, Kepler-16b enjoys double sunsets, as it circles two stars rather than a single sun. Astronomers confirmed this first discovery of what's called a "circumbinary" planet in 2011. That's thirty-four years after its fictional counterpart was dreamed up in *A New Hope*!

Kepler-16b sits in a system about 200 light-years from Earth. Its mass is similar to that of Saturn, which makes it much bigger than Tatooine, whose diameter is only 82 percent of the earth's. The Kepler-16 stars are small compared to our sun, at about 69 percent and 20 percent of the sun's mass. The two Tatoo stars are both roughly sun-sized.

The story of Kepler-16b is a good example of how planet-hunting works. Pictures captured by Kepler's camera showed two stars orbiting each other. Next, eclipses were seen, where one star moved in front of the other. But, when they took an even closer look, astronomers found that the eclipses couldn't be explained by the movement of the two stars alone. Instead, the tiny drop in light from the stars—a dimming of only 1.7 percent—was found to be the telltale sign of an orbiting planet!

Conditions on Kepler-16b

Astronomers think that Kepler-16b is far cooler than Tatooine. Down on the surface of the frosty world of Kepler-16b, a planetary explorer would feel a temperature range from −70°C to −100°C. This chilly world would never see constant daylight, as the two stars are too close together. The binaries would come together in an eclipse every 20.5 days, then move apart again. As their separation in the sky increased, they would go down at different times, in the kind of sunsets never spied on Earth but often seen on Tatooine.

Could Kepler-16b support life? Well, astronomers think that it sits in an orbit within the Goldilocks Zone. The Zone of the Kepler-16 system is from about 55 million to 106 million kilometers away from the two suns. Kepler-16b lies at an orbit of 104 million kilometers, so it sits near the outer limits of its Goldilocks Zone. But, where life is concerned, remember that this is a gas giant with freezing temperatures!

So chances of life on Kepler-16b are slim. But what about an exomoon? Sometime in its history, Kepler-16b could have captured an Earth-sized world from the center of its Goldilocks Zone. Gravity waves from other bodies in the Kepler-16 system could have caused this "earth" to migrate. That would send it on a journey that ended up with Kepler-16b, making the "earth" its moon. Space can be weird!

Life could also develop outside the Kepler-16 Zone. Astronomers think it's also possible for this system to have a planet orbiting at about 140 million kilometers away from the center. If this planet had a good and thick enough mix of gases in its atmosphere, including carbon dioxide and methane, it could keep the heat needed for liquid water on its surface.

Circumbinary Sweet Spots

These possible planets are cool and exciting. Don't forget that, for many years, astronomers said that planets could not form around binary stars, due to the effects of gravity.

But *Star Wars* ignored all that. Their storytellers put Tatooine in what's called a "circumbinary sweet spot" of the Tatoo system. In other words, planet Tatooine is just in the right place to orbit two binary stars at once. And now that Kepler-16b has been discovered, new research shows that Tatooine-type planets are not only possible but may actually be quite common. It seems there might be sweet spots in other systems. Tatooines may be common in the universe!

The Case of OGLE-2005-BLG-390Lb

That brings us to another exoplanet, discovered close to the center of our Milky Way galaxy. This Inner Rim world, as we could call it, is an earthlike planet that circles its parent star once in about ten years. The name of the planet? OGLE-2005-BLG-390Lb—don't blame me, I didn't name it! Perhaps the astronomer who did was either a little drunk, or simply fell onto his keyboard. But OGLE-2005-BLG-390Lb orbits a red star five times less massive than our sun, and is at a distance of about 20,000 light-years from us.

OGLE-2005-BLG-390Lb sounds more like Hoth than it does the earth. From space, Hoth looked like a pale blue ball, due to its cover of thick ice and snow. Hoth was the sixth planet in its system, which means the temperature, although always freezing, would drop to −60°C at night.

OGLE-2005-BLG-390Lb sounds similar. With a cool parent star and large orbit, this exoplanet has a surface temperature of about −220°C, too cold for liquid water. It's also likely to have a thin atmosphere, and a rocky surface buried under layers of ice, or beneath frozen oceans. OGLE-2005-BLG-390Lb is about five times the mass of the earth. Hoth is smaller, more like the size of Mars. In its system, OGLE-2005-BLG-390Lb sits at an average distance of two to four Earth–sun distances from its mother star. This means that in our solar system, OGLE-2005-BLG-390Lb would fall somewhere between Mars and Jupiter.

Where Your Shadow Always Has Company

NASA was quick to see how they could use exoplanets to promote the work that NASA does. In 2015, the space agency published a series of travel posters. They were created by NASA artists Joby Harris, David Delgado, and Dan Goods. Using an art deco style, bold colors, and a classic design—as used in the golden age of travel—the posters invited space tourists to visit exoplanets! The posters included one on dual-star planet Kepler-16b, which boasted the line: "where your shadow always has company."

David Delgado said they felt inspired by the discovery of so many new exoplanets: "We thought it would be really cool to explore the characteristics of each planet through the context of travel," he said. "It feels like we're living in the future, or science fiction is coming to life."

THE LINK BETWEEN HOTH AND MARS: WHY MIGHT HUMANS MAKE LIKE EXOGORTHS?

The pirate starship sits in the dark and desolate cave of an asteroid. The *Millennium Falcon* cockpit is silent, lit only by the pulsing hyperdrive lights of the flight deck. Leia sits alone in the pilot's seat. Something moves outside the cockpit window and catches her eye. With the lights reflecting in the window, it's hard to make out what's moving. She moves closer to the glass and gazes into the gloom.

For how far does this cave system run? The darkness of the cave is so black that the depths of the cave are impossible to fathom. In science fiction movies such as *The Empire Strikes Back*, alien caves are like cosmic catacombs! Sometimes they're so big that even spaceships can fly down them. On Earth, there are thousands of miles of unexplored caves. But what about the caves of our moon and of planets such as Mars? How big could they be? How long are they? And how much do we know about them? Might this dark side of our solar system be used to help colonize space?

The Moon as a Stepping-Stone

The earth's moon has been a target for us humans for many years. It's on our cosmic doorstep, so it's within easy reach of Earth. In the *Star Wars* galaxy, many of the alien species, including humans, started out on home planets in the Core Worlds. The home planet for humans was most likely to be Coruscant. We humans on Earth think about going out into space by starting with our moon. The old Coruscanti would have faced a similar kind of choice in the very early days of the exploration of *Star Wars* space.

The closeness of our moon might enable humans, living and working on the moon, to trade goods for the things they need from Earth. It would be the beginning of our own interplanetary trade routes. The moon is also a good place to set up powerful telescopes, and a stepping-stone for further exploration of our galaxy.

The NASA Apollo mission program of 1969–1972 was the work of true pioneers. The missions put a total of twelve humans on the moon and tested how we humans might cope with lunar living. Each mission was longer than the one before. We wanted to explore the moon further, and see how well the astronauts could cope while doing different sorts of experiments. The Apollo program also taught us how to take large items of equipment and materials to another world.

Make Like an Exogorth

When humans live on the moon, they will need to live a little like the exogorth in the *Star Wars* galaxy. Remember that exogorths, also known as space slugs or giant space slugs, were an alien species that lived in the caves and hollows of asteroids. We saw one such creature living in that asteroid near Hoth. Humans living on the moon might also find it useful to dwell in such caves.

Visiting the moon is one thing, but living there won't be easy. There are huge swings in temperature. It can be as hot as 134°C (273°F) at midday to –170°C (–274°F) at night. The surface of the moon is always being blasted by micro-meteorites and harmful cosmic rays. So humans can survive these conditions, they may have to live underground in lunar "lava tubes." Lunar lava tubes are underground cave tunnels on the moon. They were formed by the flow of magma in the moon's ancient past. When the surface of a lava tube cooled, and the flow of lava died down, the tunnels would become drained, making hollow catacombs and cave systems.

So it looks like the exogorths got it right. Lava tubes are a very useful living space. Many are long, natural caves, as wide as 500 meters (1,600 feet) before they start to collapse. Even if the tubes survive, the movement of the moon itself—or meteorite bombardment—may still collapse some passages. No wonder Leia was anxious about the strange, creaking noises coming from the asteroid catacombs at night.

Not all lunar living would copy the ways of the giant space slug! Mynocks are right off the menu on the moon. To be honest, the question of food and water is a major problem for lunar colonization. At first, food would need to be brought along—more than just a packed lunch, of course. But scientists think that water is hidden in the soil at the moon's south pole.

Special machines would be needed to draw the water from the ground. Growing plants will also be difficult at first. The nights can be long and cold, and the daylight bright and harsh, as there is no atmosphere on the moon to reduce and scatter the sun's radiation. There are also no insects there to pollinate the flowers. So a new way of growing food would need to be found. These are all good reasons to dwell in the caves and tunnels until better living conditions can be built.

Like the ancient Coruscanti, we humans have an outward urge to explore space. A number of nations hope to put us back on the moon. One plan is to put a farm at its northern pole. A farm here would receive eight hours of sunlight each day, throughout the lunar summer. The farm could have a special covering, providing protection—from the fierce solar radiation—and insects for pollination. But even so, a farm measuring 100 meters by 100 meters would not feed 100 people.

Missions to Mars

If the moon is the first stepping-stone for exploring our galaxy, Mars is next. We know more about Mars—the fourth planet out from the sun—than any planet other than Earth. That's because it's the closest planet whose surface we can see through our telescopes. Where our other closest neighbor, Venus, is shrouded in a veil of mysterious cloud, the Red Planet is plain to see. Like Earth, Mars has a twenty-four-hour day, it has seasons, and it has polar caps. If there's a planet we would colonize first, it would be Mars.

The Coruscant system was ripe for colonization. As well as the planet Coruscant itself, there were eleven planets in orbit about their parent star, Coruscant Prime. Before those planets could be used as stepping-stones into *Star Wars* space, Coruscant also had four moons, which could have acted as stepping-stone targets for early colonization.

For us humans, Mars has huge potential. Some scientists even think that pioneers should skip the moon and head straight for Mars. Although Mars has much in common with Earth, it still lacks some of the things we need to live, such as warmth and water. Not only that, but a Martian colony would have to deal with global dust storms and solar radiation and would have to melt the polar ice into a sea twelve meters deep, covering much of the planet. All are huge tasks to do!

So how would pioneers change Mars to meet these challenges? Lava tubes! Once more, it's easy to see how lava tubes can be used, at least until the Martian colony can truly take off. But is there a maze of Martian tunnels fit for the task?

The Telltale Sign of the Tubes

In 2007, NASA's Mars Odyssey spacecraft made a stunning discovery. Odyssey spied holes in cave roofs on the slopes of a Martian volcano. A lava tube is sometimes found by spying such telltale "skylights," a place in which the roof of the tube has collapsed and left a round hole in the surface. The Odyssey discovery excited astronomers into searching for caves and caverns elsewhere on the Red Planet.

Mars has huge volcanoes that are much bigger than the ones on Earth. The famous Martian volcano Olympus Mons reaches an impressive height of twenty-one kilometers, while the whole region of the Tharsis volcanic bulge covers a surface of over 25 million square kilometers. As gravity on Mars is much less than half of Earth's, Martian lava tubes are expected to be much larger, although they are unlikely to be hiding any exogorths!

Earthlings Become Martians

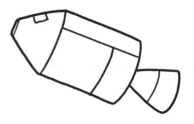

So, in the near future, parts of our solar system are ripe for colonization. Like the old Coruscanti, we should hop from planet to planet. Mars may be our first home away from home. The first launch could carry an unmanned Earth Return Vehicle (ERV) to Mars. The ERV would contain a nuclear reactor, which would power a unit to make fuel, using material found on Mars. Two years later, a manned mission would touch down near the ERV. The crew would stay for eighteen months, exploring the planet until returning to Earth using ERV-made fuel. The crew would be replaced by another team, and a string of bases would be set up.

The Martian lava tubes would act as a main base. The tubes may have the trapped water needed for life, and may have reservoirs of ancient ice, since cool air can pool in lava tubes and temperatures remain stable. If visitors from Earth make like exogorths and use the tubes as a home, in good time Mars will be transformed to become more like Earth. After several decades, the Red Planet will look as blue and watery as our home planet. Within a century, it could be changed into an oxygen-rich environment, supporting a human colony, some of whom may dream of traveling to the remote corners of the solar system and beyond.

PART III
ALIENS

WOULD AN EXOGORTH REALLY EVOLVE ON AN ASTEROID?

Movies about aliens have given us some of the best taglines of all time: "In space, no one can hear you scream." "We are not alone." And, of course, "A long time ago, in a galaxy far, far away." Science fiction writers and directors, like George Lucas and J. J. Abrams, have thought long and hard about how to portray creatures from other planets.

That's why *Star Wars* has given us a zoo-load of aliens on our movie screens. The Tusken Raiders, or Sand People, may walk like humans, but they are badass monsters that stalk the sands of Tatooine. The Hutts, Jabba and company, are an intelligent species of large gastropods. Like a bunch of alien crime lords, the Hutts have short arms, huge eyes, and wide cavernous mouths—all the better to eat you with. The Gungans, like Jar Jar Binks, are a race of amphibious humanoids native to the waters of Naboo. And each alien fits into the environment in which it lives.

Darwin Invented the Alien

It was Charles Darwin who kind of invented the modern alien we see in *Star Wars*. Darwin's famous theory of evolution gave writers and movie directors a new way of imagining how life might arise on other worlds. Before Darwin, aliens were not really extraterrestrial. They were merely humans like us, living on other planets.

But Darwin changed all that. From Darwin on, the idea of life beyond our home planet became truly alien. Aliens in stories started to have weird bodies and brains, in other words the true physical and mental traits of extraterrestrials. And that's how, through sci-fi like *Star Wars*, the idea of the alien became so popular in the human imagination.

Three kinds of alien soon became common in sci-fi stories. The alien as highly evolved killer was the first kind. For example, the Martians in *War of the Worlds* (2005), or the predatory mother monster in Ridley Scott's *Alien* (1979). The Tusken Raiders would fit into this first category.

The second kind of alien is a kind you really weren't expecting, such as an alien that is an ocean-planet! This kind was in a famous story called "Solaris," written by Stanisław Lem in 1961. "Solaris" was later made into films in 1972 and 2002. The swirling sea in "Solaris" is a single organism with a vast, yet strange, intelligence that humans try to understand. *Star Wars* has its own intelligent planet in Zonama Sekot, which can even make itself travel through space!

Thirdly, there's the kind of alien who is a wise and kind teacher of humans. The 1977 movie *Close Encounters of the Third Kind* had wise and kind aliens visiting planet Earth. And in *Star Wars*, of course, there's Yoda—a teacher who has almost infinite wisdom.

Carbon versus Silicon

But what about the exogorth? We spoke in the last chapter about this giant space slug that lived in the hollows of an asteroid in the Hoth system. The *Star Wars* legend says that the exogorth was a silicon-based species. That's the creature which was seen living in cosmic catacombs of the asteroid. Let's stop and think about that for a moment. Sci-fi writers often talk about alien life based on silicon. 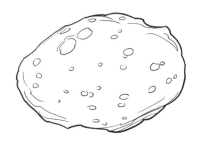 The xenomorphs from the *Alien* movies are meant to be silicon-based, for example. Silicon is a chemical similar to carbon. They sit in the same group of chemicals, and have similar properties. But carbon is the main chemical element upon which life on Earth is based. So why use silicon? The thinking goes something like this: If carbon and silicon are so similar, and carbon is a life-giver, why shouldn't silicon be the same? If you try to resist this argument about silicon, you can sometimes be accused of being biased about carbon!

But there are good reasons to be biased about carbon. Carbon is cosmic. It forms the basis of life on Earth, and is also to be found out in deep space. Carbon is the backbone of life on Earth because of its very nature. It easily bonds with life's other main elements, like hydrogen, oxygen, and nitrogen. Carbon is also light and small, making it an ideal element for creating the longer and more complicated chemicals of life, such as DNA. Carbon also makes one of the softest known substances in graphite, and one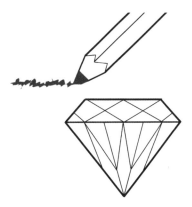

of the hardest known substances in diamond. Carbon is known to form 10 million different chemicals, which is the majority of all chemicals on Earth. Carbon is pretty versatile!

Yet, the silicon cheerleaders ask us to imagine a world on which silicon is abundant. On such a world, they say, silicon would replace carbon as the chemical for life. But there is such a world. It's called planet Earth! Silicon is more abundant than carbon on our planet's surface, and yet life here is almost always carbon-based.

Exogorth Habitat

The exogorth would have to evolve to suit the situation of the world on which it lived. How would it survive? According to *Star Wars* legend, when the exogorths become adults they are ten meters long. They produce young exogorths by splitting into two smaller, separate bodies. If an exogorth was unable to split, it would just keep on growing, and could even grow to 900 meters in length! Exogorths of this size are said to have swallowed spaceships whole.

Exogorths often lurk in asteroid fields. They burrow into an asteroid until completely hidden. In the darkness, they feed on a sun's energy, minerals within the asteroid, and floating space debris (though it's unclear where all the space junk actually comes from). Asleep most of the time, the exogorth welcomes any chance to lunge at a passing ship. But lunging also uses up energy, which can make the exogorth a very sad and tired slug.

On Earth, we also have creatures that exist underground, surviving on a diet of rock and water. Some asteroids are thought to have a thin coating of frost, as well as having periods in the past where their insides had become molten. But it's unlikely the inside of an asteroid would have remained melted long enough for life to emerge.

Perhaps we should pay more attention to Han Solo's remark that anyone would be crazy to follow him into an asteroid field. Maybe his words show that past victims of the asteroid field had been swallowed whole by lurking exogorths! It's even possible that the wreck of other spaceships had smashed into the smith-

ereens that made up the space junk in the exogorth diet. But that kind of diet wouldn't have given the exogorth those massive teeth. Those gnashers would come from the exogorth's diet of munching on other creatures, such as Mynocks. These were a species of silicon-based bat-like parasites. Mynocks chewed on the power cables of starships and, like the exogorths, could survive the vacuum of space.

Water Bears!

On Earth, we have our own creature that can survive the vacuum of space, the tar-digrade, or water bear. Tardigrades are indestructible. They don't look too cool,

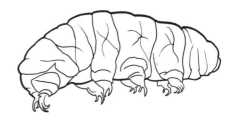

with sofa-like bodies and four pairs of stubby legs. They're nowhere near as big as exogorths, or even as massive as a Mynock. Tardigrades vary in size from 0.012 to 0.020 inches, though the largest may even reach 0.047 inches! Scientists have found tardigrades on top of Mount Everest, in hot springs, under layers of solid ice, and in ocean beds.

Tardigrades are able to survive the most extreme environments, which would kill almost every other animal. They've survived temperatures as hot as 151°C, and as cold as −272°C. They can go without water for ten years. They can stand 1,000 times more radiation than other animals. And they've even been known to survive the vacuum of space. For ten days in 2007, tardigrades were taken aboard the Foton-M3 mission into low Earth-orbit. There, they were exposed to the hard vacuum of outer space. Did that faze them? Not in the slightest. On their return to Earth, and after rehydration, most of the tardigrades recovered within thirty minutes!

So it may be wise not to write off the exogorth. Writers and directors, as well as scientists, are pushing the boundaries of imagining how life might arise and survive in space. In a universe where Zonama Sekot can travel freely through space, why shouldn't a giant space slug survive by feasting on rock and metal?

HOW COULD REY SURVIVE ON THE DESERT PLANET OF JAKKU?

The planet Jakku. The metal hatch of a junked space vessel is snatched open. We see the blue-lit, mummified face of an alien scavenger. The scavenger is decked out in bug-eyed goggles and gloves, with a face covered by a kaffiyeh.

As the camera pulls back, we get a full-bodied look at this alien scavenger. It is well equipped. Its expedition backpack has a full-length combat staff strapped on. The scavenger seems tooled up for every task. We are in an upside-down corridor. The scavenger finds a precious piece of treasure-junk, and drops it in a satchel. The satchel is swung back and the scavenger climbs down a cable, flanked by huge walls of machinery.

The scavenger looks so alone and elfin in this gargantuan space of a sideways shipwreck. The alien drops down the 200-foot cable, landing hard on rusted metal, and heads out through the rust-dust toward a slit of sunlight. Emerging from the machine darkness, the scavenger pulls off the bug eyes. What's revealed is the face of a beautiful, young female humanoid. She holds a canteen to her lips and shakes the last drops of water into her mouth.

It's Rey. The camera cuts wide, to show a tiny Rey set against the epic engine of a crashed star destroyer. Rey sets off down a sand dune and onto the salt flats below. Her speeder is dwarfed against a graveyard of wrecked starships, as she sputters to a remote outpost of civilization.

Jakku

Jakku is an isolated desert world. It sits in the Western reaches of the *Star Wars* galaxy. It is a hostile planet in which Rey survives. Deserts are places of extreme climate, where heat exhaustion is a real threat, and where rainfall is often less than ten inches in a year. A harsh and desert planet like Jakku is only survivable by the hardiest of humans, such as Rey.

How does this planet of Jakku compare with Earth? Jakku is a desert world of dry, sandy landscapes, scorching skies, and hot temperatures. On Earth, we have deserts such as the Sahara in North Africa, which is part of a desert band that runs through the Middle East and into South and Central Asia. The driest place on Earth is the Atacama Desert in South America. Some parts of the Atacama have never seen rain. The high mountains that divide the Atacama from the Amazon jungle drain the rain clouds. All the rain falls on the mountains, which means that Atacama sits in what's called a rain shadow.

Like Jakku, Earth also has sand dunes. Our home planet has dunes on the coast and inland dunes, desert dunes, which are laid out in pretty patterns. There are even sand dunes on Mars. Both planets have the kind of towering sand dunes that Rey rode down to the salt flats. Sand is made from the erosion of rocks. Through wind and over time, a dune can grow to a mountain a thousand feet high. Dunes are like skyscrapers in sand. And dunes are not just stacks of lifeless sand. They are structures of nature that shift, grow, and travel. And they are teeming with life!

For Rey, sandboarding on Jakku would have been the same as that on Earth or Mars. Sandboarding is like snowboarding; same board, different surface. Sand is lighter than snow, so boarders get a swifter ride than they would on snow. You can sandboard with your snowboard, or you can buy a sandboard, which has a base like glass. Rey made do with sheet metal. It was a way of getting down the sand dune slickly.

A sand dune can swallow you whole. So, for Rey, sandboarding would not have been just for fun. Loose sand can be deadly. And old dunes can collapse unexpectedly. Most of the time, it's safe to make your way across the miles of endless dunes. Although on Jakku, it is always a good idea to be well equipped, and tell someone of your plans. Especially if you're going through the Sinking Fields in the Goazon Badlands. The fields were north of Rey's AT-AT home, and they were the site of the crash landing by Poe Dameron after he escaped the First Order's flagship, Finalizer. Soon after impact, the fields swallowed Poe's TIE fighter whole, to the horror of Finn.

Surviving the Desert

Rey had a limited chance of survival in the desert. Her main challenges were the heat and the few resources available. Shelter and water were scarce. Food could be hard to find, as many creatures hid from the heat in the daytime. Vegetated areas (known as wadis on Earth), grassed plains, and higher ground were more promising places for survival. Wadis may hold water from what rain may have fallen, and higher ground usually meant colder temperatures, as well as good places for visibility. But the greatest danger came from dehydration and heat exhaustion. Rey kept water on her at all times.

There was also the possibility of predators, such as the ripper-raptor and the Arconan night terror. The ripper-raptor was a species of flying reptile, with leathery wings and keen eyesight. It was a perfect creature for the vast plains of Jakku. Ripper-raptors were flesh-eaters that rode the thermal winds in the deep of the desert in the Kelvin Ravine. They tried to pick off people from the settlement of Tuanul. The Arconan night terror, also known as the nightwatcher worm, was a sand-specimen with large red eyes, and a body that could reach twenty meters in length. On Jakku, scavenger tales told of nightwatchers lying motionless under the sand, only to spring and snap at prey at the tiniest vibration on the surface. So Rey made sure she was always armed and ready.

Making Ends Meet

Rey would have been drawn to the steelpecker. We see it in an early scene in *The Force Awakens* as Rey's speeder first sputters across the sands. The steelpecker was a carrion bird with beak and talons tipped with iron. They fed mainly on metal, which meant their digestive systems stored metals in their gizzards! All this made the steelpecker a very useful treasure to scavengers like Rey, who collected their carcasses and guano.

But Rey had better ways of making ends meet. Jakku was a planet that was used as a jumping-off point for warships heading west, into the Unknown Regions. At peak times, such as the Galactic Civil War, this meant increased traffic and, if scavengers were lucky, more wrecked starships. Even if the wreckage was found far away from settlements such as Tuanul, Cratertown, or Reestkii, luggabeasts could be used to carry supplies across the desert to Niima Outpost, a trading post and the only major settlement on the planet.

Junked engine parts can easily be made into something new. Just look at the way Anakin built an entire podracer from junked parts. So, Rey would scrub her day's salvage clean, and trade it with her blobfish boss, Unkar Plutt, for sealed packets of dried green meat or powdered bread.

Desert Planet Study

A couple of questions to finish up. Firstly, is it really possible to have a whole planet consisting of sand? And second, is it really possible to survive on such a planet? A 2011 research project found that not only are desert planets possible, but they may even be more common than earthlike planets. The models that scientists made in the study showed that desert planets had a much larger Goldilocks Zone than watery planets. The study also said that Venus may once have been a habitable desert planet, as recently as a billion years ago. And that the earth may become a desert planet within a billion years, because our sun is getting hotter. Maybe we'd better pay more attention to Rey's survival skills!

ARE THERE SIMPLY TOO MANY ALIENS IN *STAR WARS*?

The *Millennium Falcon* drops out of light speed and lands on the lush blue-green planet of Takodana. Takodana sits on the trade routes between the Inner and Outer Rim. And so, long ago, it became a popular departure point for those heading out to the galaxy's edge—Takodana was a last taste of civilization. So you can understand why the local cantina is like a shop of little horrors. It's full of rough alien travelers who gamble, drink, and scheme. Famous American film critic Roger Ebert said a *Star Wars* movie often had an "incredible collection of extraterrestrial alcoholics and bug-eyed martini drinkers lined up at the bar." And Roger said the aliens were so human that he found himself feeling admiration and delight.

In *The Force Awakens*, we see a tiny 1,000-year-old female alien wearing large, adjustable goggles. This is Maz Kanata, bug-eyed pirate-queen boss of the bizarre cantina. That saloon in Maz's castle on Takodana reminds us of just how full of alien life is the *Star Wars* galaxy. But isn't *Star Wars* being a bit optimistic about the diversity of life in the universe? And do we have a way of figuring out how much life there may be in our own galaxy?

The Drake Equation

First up, one scientific way of figuring out how much life there may be in our galaxy is the Drake Equation. The equation is named after American astronomer Frank Drake. And, whether or not you like math, we're just going to have to go through it! The equation looks like this:

$$N = R^* \times fp \times ne \times fl \times fi \times fc \times L$$

where:

N = the number of civilizations in our galaxy with which communication may be possible

R^* = the average rate of star formation per year in our galaxy

fp = the fraction of those stars that have planets

ne = the average number of planets that can potentially support life per star that has planets

fl = the fraction of planets that actually develop life

fi = the fraction of planets with life on which intelligence arises

fc = the fraction of civilizations that develop detectable signs of communication in space

L = the length of time such civilizations send detectable signals into space

The idea is this. To find out how many alien civilizations in our galaxy can communicate across space, you have to estimate each of the factors in the equation, then multiply them together. Simple!

Let's Do an Alien Head Count

Okay, roughly speaking, the first five factors on the right-hand side of the equals sign of the Drake equation (R^*, fp, ne, fl, and fi) are mostly questions of fact. The last two factors (fc and L) are more about human affairs on our planet, and are not so easy to work out.

Better than ever before, experts are in a good position to attach numbers to those first five factors. In 1977, science knew of no planets in orbit around other stars. It wasn't even very aware of the gas giant worlds in our own outer solar system. Even in 1999, the year the *Star Wars* prequels hit the cinema screens, scientists were aware of only a limited number of gas giants around other stars. But today, thanks to NASA's Kepler space probe, experts estimate there may be as many as 4.5 billion earthlike planets in orbit around just the red dwarf stars in our galaxy.

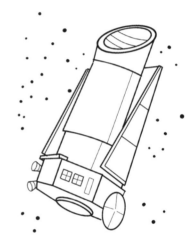

Yet, there's still a problem with those five factors of the Drake equation. Two different scientists, both using the same data sets, can reach very different results. Those results can even be as different as this: One scientist would believe the data showed that *Star Wars* is right—our galaxy is indeed also full of aliens. We just haven't met up with them yet. Or maybe they're on the other side of our galaxy. But the second scientist believes the data shows we're alone in the universe!

Aliens in Space and Time

But when scientists do come to an agreement, something fascinating emerges. It's this: When all the "best guess" data has been factored into the Drake equation, the number of alien civilizations in our galaxy (N) turns out almost equal to their average lifetime in years (L).

For example, say a typical alien society lasts for only 100 years. Then there will only be roughly 100 of them in the galaxy. In which case, your chance of meeting up with Balosars, Mynocks, and bug-eyed monsters is pretty slim, but if alien civilizations last a good 10,000 years, the data says there will be roughly 10,000 such civilizations, and alien contact is a much better bet!

So let's think again about that vast ocean of a *Star Wars* galaxy. It has around 20 million species living in it. And according to the data, that means that the average lifetime of an alien civilization in *Star Wars* is 20 million years. That seems like a long time, but remember—the universe is 13,000 million years old. Maybe the *Star Wars* writers have faith in alien intelligence. Perhaps they believe that intelligent beings can get past the politics of greed and don't pollute their home planets or fall for the politics of war and don't blow each other up. So there really could have been aliens living a long, long time ago, in a galaxy, far, far away.

HOW COME MANY PLANETS IN *STAR WARS* HAVE BREATHABLE ATMOSPHERES?

Humans, lost in space. A group of colonists left their home planet of Grizmallt and headed out to the stars. They lost their way in the Mid Rim, close to the border of the Outer Rim Territories. But they were lucky enough to crash on a small lush-green planet whose surface was a stunning range of different landscapes. Rolling plains, grassy hills, and swamplands under the cloud cover of the forever-gray twilight side of the planet.

This was Naboo. The human colonists from Grizmallt went to Naboo's Gallo Mountains, and started farming at the Dee'ja Peak. Colonizing other planets in the *Star Wars* galaxy seems to have been a piece of (moist) Gungan cake. No need for lava tubes, like on our moon or Mars. No need to get used to the place. And no need for breathing devices. You simply crash-landed and, bingo, before you know it, you're running a farm on a perfect-looking planet. You can even eat the local delicacies.

Is life in the *Star Wars* galaxy really that simple? How come so many planets have such clean air and breathable atmospheres?

How Breathable Planets Are Made

The air we breathe on planet Earth today is made by a number of factors. Gravity and geography, sunlight and seas, and, of course, by Earth's animal and plant life. Some of these factors are local. Others are more global. With so many factors, it's easy to see why the weather is hard to forecast in some places. And it's also easy to see why the "air" of other worlds could be so very different from our own breathable air.

Our story of Earth's air starts way back. The original Earth of 4.6 billion years ago would have been slowly forming out of the gases swarming around the newborn Sun. In time, the gases became liquids and solids. Some cooled to start the seas, some became the rocky continents. But the very core of the earth continued to stay hot, which still makes our home a live planet.

And above it all, like a sock around the surface of this living planet, sits the air. Scientists think the original air of the early earth escaped into space. Compared to today's breathable air, this early air was poisonous—rich in gases like ammonia, neon, and methane. There was little or no oxygen. But then, microscopic life arose and breathed oxygen into the air. That changed the air of the earth forever. Over many millions of years, the air changed into the air we breathe today.

As it was on Earth, so it would be on planets in the *Star Wars* galaxy. Wherever planets grow and change, the same thing happens. Air evolves. So we might expect the air of a planet like Naboo to be different from the air of a desert world like Jakku. And both would be different from the air of an icy world like Hoth—different geography, different life-forms, and likely different gravity. There'll also be different levels of sunlight on each world. That depends on the planet's distance from its mother star.

Oceans will play a part, too. Only 8 percent of Endor's surface was covered with water. Compare that with 71 percent of Earth's, and Kamino—the *Star Wars* world where the clone army for the Galactic Republic was created—was entirely water!

The Colonizing Coruscanti

But, when you think about it, *Star Wars* isn't saying that all planets in its galaxy have breathable air. It's only those planets where humans live. We just don't see a huge number of planets with poisonous air. Humans like Han and Leia don't visit those wayward worlds. Humans wouldn't have settled there in the first place. Not unless the planet had been transformed. If Naboo hadn't been breathable, its early human colonists would have had no tale to tell. They would simply have perished in the poisonous air. They would have left the planet to the Gungans. And we do sometimes catch a glimpse of worlds with unbreathable atmospheres, such as the gas giants Endor and Yavin, which we see from space.

How would humans have found planets with breathable atmospheres in the *Star Wars* galaxy? The *Star Wars* stories say that the human population began with the Coruscanti. Their home world sat near the center of the galaxy. That's a perfect place from which to explore the densely packed core of the *Star Wars* stories. So, out of their home world the Coruscanti came, in their sleek spaceships. They would have found their part of the galaxy full of other stars. And around those stars orbited many planets. Of those planets, what number would have been habitable?

On November 4, 2013, Earth scientists said there could be as many as 40 billion earthlike planets in our Milky Way galaxy. Some say there are around 500 sun-like stars within 100 light-years of our solar system. And the core of the *Star Wars* galaxy would be 500 times more densely packed than that. So plenty of candidate planets for colonizing.

From their spaceships, the Coruscanti could sample candidate planets from afar. They could use an onboard remote-sensing kit for any telltale signs of whether the planet had "good air." Many worlds, of course, would already have been inhabited by other creatures. Yet more worlds—those found to be poisonous to humans—could be terraformed. Terraforming means "earth-shaping," or in the case of *Star Wars*, we might call it "Coruscant-converting." It's the way in which a moon, planet, or other body is controlled in terms of its temperature, air, and geography to change into a version of planet Earth—or Coruscant!—to make it fit for human life.

So with that Mos Eisley cantina in mind, *Star Wars* may not be exaggerating about how many planets in that galaxy have breathable atmospheres. For every planet on which humans can breathe, there are millions of others on which they can't!

HOW WOULD LIFE DEVELOP IN THE *STAR WARS* GALAXY?

What makes up a Wookiee? What kind of blood flowed through the veins of Yoda? What was the history of the Hutts? The laws of science are said to be true for all corners of the cosmos. Planets, stars, and galaxies come and go in the same way they would in our local solar neighborhood. But what biology on Earth would also be true in *Star Wars*?

If we look at the alien life-forms in *Star Wars*, we find creatures we recognize, especially the ones that look humanoid. We also see much that is very alien to us. But is there anything about life in the universe, including our galaxy and the *Star Wars* galaxy, that is true for all life? Okay, maybe life on another planet is based on silicon, rather than carbon. And maybe they swim in methane, rather than water. But is there something far more basic that is common to life everywhere?

Evolution and Replication

Little about life in *Star Wars* can be understood without the idea of evolution. The history of the *Star Wars* galaxy must have been a long one, as our own history has been shown by evolution to be not only complicated, but big. Once we knew the earth was old, and that all had been created by a series of changes, we started to see that the story of our planet was part of an even older tale.

Everywhere you looked in *Star Wars*, you would see evolution. The planets, stars, and galaxy all change over time. They are systems of matter in motion. The electrons that swarm around the heart of the galaxy's atoms are part of the hydrogen and helium gas from which the stars are made. The galaxy's stars grow out of the gas, as young planets form around the young suns, such as Jakku, Ileenium, and the Endors.

But do we know what aspect of life elsewhere would be common with life on Earth? The answer is most likely to be this: replication. To replicate something means to copy it. On planet Earth, all life evolves through the survival of organisms that make copies of themselves. How do they do this? By using a chemical that we might call a replicator (calling it a copier would sound less scientific). On our home planet, the replicator that does the job is called DNA.

DNA has been called the most incredible chemical on Earth. DNA, or deoxyribonucleic acid, exists just to make more DNA. There's nearly two meters of DNA squeezed into almost every human cell. Each length of DNA has about 3.2 billion letters of coding. That's enough to enable 103,480,000,000 possible combinations. That's a huge number of possibilities. If something like DNA existed in the *Star Wars* galaxy—and we will soon argue that it would have—the possibilities are almost endless. It would mean the potential people who could have been in the place of Luke

Skywalker, but who never saw the light of Tatoo, outnumber the sand grains of Jakku. Such unborn ghosts include greater philosophers than Yoda and pilots greater than Han Solo. That's because the parade of possible people allowed by replicators like DNA hugely outnumbers the parade of actual people.

Imagine Princess Leia, looking into a mirror. If her biology works anything like ours, then she is gazing at 10,000 trillion cells. Almost every one of those cells has two yards of jam-packed DNA or some other replicator. If it were all spun into a single thread, it would make a single strand long enough to reach the moon and back, many times over.

In fact, humans are just vehicles for DNA. We are carriers of DNA. The very purpose of life is DNA survival. But DNA is not floating free. It's locked up in living bodies. And though we couldn't live without it, DNA itself is not alive. In fact, it's very unreactive. That's why it survives and can be teased out of the prehistoric bones of ancient warriors. It's curious that something so lifeless should be at the very core of life on Earth and maybe elsewhere.

The Cipher of Life

The river of DNA flows through time. It's a river of data, rather than blood and bones. Most of the DNA is redundant—about 97 percent of it. But the genes, the business end of DNA, are the short sections that control our vital functions. Genes have been compared to the keys of a piano, each playing only a single note. And the combination of genes,

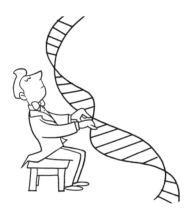

like the combination of piano keys, creates chords and a vast variety of tunes. The total set of genes is known as the genome. The human genome is like a kind of instruction manual for our bodies.

What would the replicator have been in the *Star Wars* galaxy? Experiments here on Earth show that it's possible to change features of our DNA. So, not only do alternatives to DNA exist, but scientists also think it's possible to make a kind of super-DNA. And this much more powerful replicator, what we might call "*Star Wars* DNA," could create very different results.

So we have our answer. Replicators like DNA may not be limited to Earth. The origin of life on *Star Wars* planets may have a lot in common with that on Earth. This is especially true if those planets had lots of water. But the actual evolution of life in the *Star Wars* galaxy would have gone very differently than it did on Earth. That's why there would be no dinosaurs on D'Qar, and no Neanderthals on Naboo. Not unless they were taken there from Earth, but that sounds like a plot from Episode XXXVII.

COMETS AND EWOKS: HOW DOES EVOLUTION GO IN *STAR WARS*?

Is there one image from *The Force Awakens* that shows us how tough life can be in the *Star Wars* galaxy? Yes, it has to be Rey's struggle to survive on Jakku, with no family to support her. This is the feature of evolution we are used to talking about. The struggle for survival that all species have, even if they're human. But there are other features of evolution. On the scale of microscopes, random changes in DNA means creatures can get lucky just by being born. And on the scale of telescopes, cosmic catastrophes can happen to planets that makes life extinct. Even creatures as successful as dinosaurs can die out, if a big space rock just happens to hit your planet.

Humans on Earth are at risk from all three features of evolution. So far, scientists have only studied biology here on our planet. But if evolution is the same on all planets, then the *Star Wars* galaxy would also have these same three features of change. How might that work? Let's take a look-see at evolution on Endor and Coruscant.

Natural Selection 101

Before we travel to those two *Star Wars* planets, let's remind ourselves of Charles Darwin's case for evolution. His theory had three main ideas. The first was "variation." What is variation? Ever notice that each and every human is a little bit different? It's the same with all creatures: individual members of any species are different. That's variation. Sure, Wookiees may all look the same, but each has a unique set of traits and characteristics.

Darwin's second idea is "multiplicity." What is multiplicity? Making lots of babies. Living creatures, including aliens, make more offspring and have bigger broods than their habitat can handle. So, in our galaxy and in that galaxy far, far away, the going gets tough. Creatures live in habitats in which only a small fraction of the Ewoks and Exogorths that are born actually manage to survive and dodge predators long enough to mate (assuming there's anything that can actually eat an exogorth! But don't forget Qui-Gon Jinn's famous quote from *The Phantom Menace*—"there's always a bigger fish").

The third idea was "natural selection." What's natural selection? It's the process in nature that means the types of animals that survive are those best able to produce young in the habitat in which they live, the ones that best "fit" their environment, often by sheer luck.

Cedar Forest from the Trees?

So, welcome to Darwin's world of change. Whether it's Earth or Endor, natural selection is like a kind of engine of nature, one that drives the creation of new species. As we have seen, nature favors variation. And it also favors species that are more spread around the map. The more a species is scattered, the less it relies on a single habitat. So what about those Ewoks, stuck in their famous forests? They've evolved from a line of successful ancestors. If they hadn't, they wouldn't have survived to tell the tale! But how did their habitat shape their history? And how well do they fit their environment?

Let's think a bit more about the Ewoks. This species of furry bipeds stood at an average height of about one meter tall. Like humans, Ewoks had an opposable thumb. That means Ewoks have thumbs that can be put opposite the fingers of the same hand, so that objects can be picked up and held. Opposable thumbs meant Ewoks could use  tools as well as weapons, such as spears and slings. When first found by the Empire, Ewoks were still stuck in the Stone Age. Their tech was very basic. But they were skilled in forest survival and could even use hang gliders as vehicles.

So it looks like Ewoks were hunter-gatherers. In the past, all humans were hunter-gatherers. We lived by hunting and collecting wild food, rather than farming. Farming came later. Ewoks had fire, pottery, and flight. They spent most of their time in the treetops, in villages built between the closely spaced trees. Or else they went onto the forest floor to gather and hunt.

Why were Ewoks still hunter-gatherers? Maybe they hadn't mastered metal. Metal was important for human progress on Earth. The invention of metal brought the Bronze Age civilizations. Bronze is an alloy of copper and tin. Later came the Iron Age. Both these metal ages were important stages in human evolution.

Stone-Age Sanctuary Moon

The age of metals doesn't seem to have started on Endor. Most metals, apart from gold and tiny amounts of copper, are not found in their pure state. That's why ancient humans first used tiny amounts of gold and copper for ornaments and jewelry only. There's no sign of metal jewelry on the Ewoks. It's all twine and leather. The state of the Ewok forests also suggests they've not mastered metal. In prehistoric times, Britain had been almost completely covered in woods. Yet, by the end of the 1500s, 90 percent of the ancient forests were gone, sacrificed for the sake of making metal things. Ewok trees still stand.

Okay, maybe there are no metals on the Sanctuary Moon? This doesn't seem very likely. If the Endor system is anything like our solar system, metals will exist. When stars like our sun and Endor I and II were made, the rocky inner planets were made mostly of metal cores and rocky crusts. In a similar way, Endor is also likely to have rocky surfaces and metal. So, all things considered, Ewoks stuck in the Stone Age makes the most sense.

Cosmic Catastrophe on Coruscant?

What about cosmic catastrophes in the *Star Wars* galaxy? Do planets suffer the same kind of huge impact events from comets and asteroids that Earth has in its ancient past? The earth is about 4.5 billion years old. The earliest life on our planet dates from around 3.5 billion years ago. But there's also evidence of life in graphite, which is 3.7 billion years old, as well as the remains of life found in rocks 4.1 billion years old. Life on Earth didn't really get started for around half a billion years. Until then, our planet was being bombarded by huge amounts of cosmic debris during the forming of the solar system.

Even after life had started on Earth, impacts from comets and asteroids played a major role in our history. Impacts were an important factor in many mass extinction events recorded in our planet's past. The death of the dinosaurs is the most famous example. But there are many others. The same is true of Earth's future. It's clear that impacts on Earth will continue to occur.

Were there comets and catastrophes on Coruscant too? Probably. During the Clone Wars, a Republican detail, accompanied by a D-Squad of astromech droids, saw a comet storm near the planet Abafar, a remote desert planet located in the Outer Rim Territories. And, ages before the Battle of Endor, a comet named Kinro was about to destroy several Core planets. But the comet itself was destroyed before it reached the Mid Rim. Its destruction was accomplished by the Jedi Order, who banded together and used the Force to break the comet apart. Several Jedi lost their lives or minds as the drama unfolded.

But is there something fishy about the science of this story? The Core worlds (also known as the Coruscant Core) includes Alderaan, Corellia, Hosnian Prime, and Coruscant itself. But the Mid Rim is a region of the

Star Wars galaxy located between the Expansion Region and the Outer Rim Territories. In other words, the Mid Rim is light-years—to say the least—away from the Core worlds. Is it possible to have a comet that moves between stars, as suggested by *Star Wars*?

Yes. Such comets are thought to exist. They're ejected from their home systems. Maybe by the gravity from nearby planets, or perhaps by passing stars. Kinro would have to have met with some serious forces to make its way from beyond the Mid Rim to where it was destroyed. Sounds like the work of dark forces!

PART IV
TECH

HOW MIGHT A *STAR WARS* SPEEDER WORK?

Go on, admit it. You've imagined yourself on a *Star Wars* speeder, haven't you? Maybe in your dreams you fly through the forests of Endor. Or maybe, like Rey, you glide over the sands of Jakku in a scratch-built speeder. Speeders in *Star Wars* look like rocket-powered hover-scooters. But their engines can reach speeds up to 310 miles per hour. So speeder pilots need to be skilled, as the high velocity can mean less safety for the pilots.

But how do speeders work? If they were like hovercraft on Earth, then the way they'd work would be simple. They'd need just three things: a platform, a motorized fan, and a large skirt of material to trap air under the craft. The air cushion under the hovercraft makes a ring of air, which runs around the base of the skirt. This keeps the air from escaping and, bingo, the craft hovers! All you need do is propel and steer. But how exactly would you propel it?

Luke's X-34 landspeeder was propelled by using three air-cooled thrust turbines, which sit at the back of his speeder. But there's no skirt in sight. Another example would be the 614-AvA speeder, the Lothal speeder bike used by the Imperial army. Or the 74-Z speeder bikes used in the Battle of Endor. Sure, they look sleek. But they're made of just a seat and steerage shaft, along with tail fins and stirrups. Not much hovering going on there!

And maglev is unlikely to be the way speeders work too. What's maglev? It's short for magnetic levitation. If you've ever played with magnets, you know that opposite magnetic poles repel, right? That's the basic idea behind magnetic levitation. Using powerful electromagnets, a maglev train, for example, floats on a magnetic field that sits between train and track. But there's no track in the woods of Endor, and no rail in sight on the sands of Jakku.

Remember that scene where Han Solo's frozen body floats through the corridors of Cloud City? Now that's as cool as carbonite. Perhaps this scene is another clue to the mystery of speeder power. There's something special going on in the science of *Star Wars*. And get this: when Luke parks his landspeeder and switches off its engine, it continues to float just like the carbonited Han!

The *Star Wars* secret is repulsorlift. Repulsorlift was a technology that enabled a craft to hover, or even fly. They did this above the surfaces of planets by pushing against gravity. So, many people have assumed this *Star Wars* repulsorlift engine design was an antigravity device.

Antigravity

Antigravity is one of the great dreams of sci-fi. Antigravity is the idea of a force that is opposite to gravity. The idea first emerged in the late 1800s. Back then, sci-fi writers imagined devices that would allow people—or objects— to hover, or to be boosted about. We owe the most famous antigravity device to British sci-fi writer H. G. Wells. His book *The First Men in the Moon* describes how antigravity shutters made of "cavorite," a metal that shields against gravity, are used to send rockets to the moon.

When we take a closer look at *Star Wars*, we see antigravity devices everywhere. Not only with Luke's speeder on Tatooine and the sleek speeders on Endor, but also with Jabba's *Khetanna*. The *Khetanna* is a massive sail barge, with a crew of twenty-six and a capacity of 500 passengers. Also, let's not forget the frozen and floating Han, or the Single Trooper Aerial Platform (STAP) vehicles piloted by single battle droids.

Repulsorlift

So in *Star Wars*, repulsorlift is king. We can assume that, like in the sci-fi stories of old, *Star Wars* craft use an antigravity invention to float in the air. It looks effortless, too. Just picture Luke's parked speeder, or every single craft lined up for the start of the pod race in *The Phantom Menace*. They float with ease, resisting the planet's gravity as if it simply didn't exist. How do they stay at a certain height above a planet's surface? Well, the speeder, or any type of craft, would need to apply an equal and opposite push to the downward gravity force of the planet (the idea of balanced forces is one from the British scientist Isaac Newton). And if the craft needed to accelerate upward on the planet, it would need to apply an even greater force (another idea of Newton's).

Now according to Albert Einstein, gravity is just curved space. So, all that's needed to create antigravity is to simply bend space the other way. And if space can be bent this way, then you not only have antigravity but also the ability to float freely and to shoot across the sky!

But how would you do it? Well, massive objects make gravity, and there's plenty of mass in the universe. But is there some material that makes antigravity? Some scientists think they have spotted a good candidate: exotic matter. What's exotic matter? It's matter that has negative mass. In other words, it's matter whose mass is of the opposite sign to the mass of normal matter. So, for example, a mass of exotic matter would be -4 pounds, rather than $+4$ pounds. Scientists hope that exotic matter will create the reverse effect of gravity, so it could be used to cancel out the weight of a speeder, or any repulsorlift craft.

Let's Build a Speeder

Imagine you're some kind of engineering wizard, like the wunderkind Anakin Skywalker. You've mastered pod racing, and your next pet project is your own personal speeder. You've done your sleek and retro design. Your speeder looks like something from a 1950s sci-fi movie. You know the kind of thing: a futuristic look, with Perspex windshield and go-faster tail fins.

But the crucial bit of the build is repulsorlift. Just how much exotic matter do you add to the mix? You simply measure the mass of your craft and pop into the speeder an equal mass of the exotic stuff. Bingo, the mass of your speeder is canceled out. Now, with no mass, your speeder won't be pulled down by the planet or repulsed from it. When you park it, just like Luke, your speeder will rest at whatever height you left it. With thrusters on board, too, you're now free to roam the skies!

You can also imagine more complex builds. Think of Sebulba's huge pod racer, Jabba's *Khetanna*, or even the repulsorpods—the hovering balconies for members of the Galactic Senate. To cancel any extra mass in each case (including passengers), you'd simply need to add the same amount of exotic matter. This would stop *Khetanna* from sinking into the sand and the delegates from falling down into the debating chamber.

One last detail remains: What exactly is exotic matter? Trouble is, no one really knows, right now. Roughly speaking, it's matter *not* made of subatomic particles such as protons and neutrons. Exotic matter is simply made of different stuff. We're just not sure what that stuff might be. Yet.

STORMTROOPER UNIFORMS: IS THAT WHY THEY'RE SUCH TERRIBLE SHOTS?

Star Wars movies often win awards for costume design. In these days of CGI, moviemakers can do almost anything with makeup and costume. So what does *Star Wars* do that is so special? Maybe it's the cavalry/cowboy style of Han Solo. Or maybe it's the robot design of C-3PO. The style of C-3PO takes its inspiration from another robot, a female robot called Maria in the 1927 sci-fi movie classic *Metropolis*. Or perhaps it's Darth Vader: his evil is all the scarier due to the mystery of his faceless helmet.

The real award winners in the sci-fi fashion stakes are the *Star Wars* stormtroopers. American fashion magazine *Vogue* even named the stormtrooper suits in their top ten *Star Wars* catwalk costumes. But have these fashion journalists actually tried to wear the stormtrooper suit? It's high time they did! So let's have a look at what they might look forward to. Let's lift the lid on what life might be like inside one of those suits, with its challenges at work, rest, and play.

Bedecked Like a Buckethead

First up, what were the stormtroopers actually wearing? The official stormtrooper armor was a white plastoid material worn over a black body glove (a kind of body suit which clings to the wearer). The armor was said to be the best in the Empire and was dreaded by rebel freedom fighters.

The suit was made up of eighteen overlapping plates and was accompanied by synthetic leather boots, which made the wearer more mobile. A sniper knee-protector plate sat over the wearer's left knee. This helped improve shooting when crouched in a sniper's position. Now this seems to assume that all stormtroopers are right-handed shots! But we can suppose that the sniper plate can be pulled off and placed on the right knee too. The suit also helped protect the wearer from glancing blaster bolts. Note the word "glancing" here. No mention is made of point-blank shots.

It's not just humans that wore stormtrooper suits. Sure, the great majority were fitted for humans and yet other forms were made to suit other species. The idea of Yoda suited up in this way is quite amusing. But surely, the sheer bulk of Jabba the Hutt would force any suit to the breaking point.

A soft click would tell the wearer whether they had attached the armor correctly. The suit makers promise that the armor was protection from most weapons and blast shrapnel. (That's some pretty tough composite plastoid, right there.) But they do admit that the suit made running difficult, and was not so good if directly hit by Cyclers (rifles that fired solid projectiles) and blasters, whenever the hit was not "glancing." The suit makers don't mention the crotch plate. This plate could prove tricky in times of urgent need to use the bathroom, especially as there's also the black body glove to deal with!

Buckethead in the Field

Once out in the field, stormtroopers could be confident in their kit. According to the suit makers anyhow. The armor would protect its recruit in extreme environments. This included the forests of Endor, the deserts of Tatooine, the icy wastelands of Hoth, and the vacuum of space, just for a short time, and in case recruits found themselves adrift, or falling from the Death Star and down into the forests of the Sanctuary Moon. It's not clear if the suit would survive an impact on the moon from that height. That would surely depend on the Jabba suit test! The secret to the suit being used in all these environments is this: The armor's plating had controls on its midsection, so the suit's temperature could be controlled.

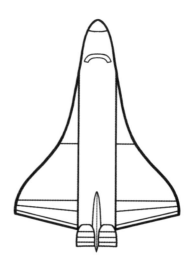

The stormtrooper suit isn't a million miles away from an astronaut suit. The Extravehicular Mobility Unit (EMU) was used by crewmembers on NASA's space shuttles and by members of the International Space Station crew. The EMU protects the astronauts from the dangers of space and worlds other than Earth. The EMU has about fifteen different layers, including smart materials, such as GORE-TEX and Kevlar. The EMU protects the astronaut's body from contact with space junk, micrometeoroids, and radiation. And, like the stormtrooper suit, the EMU is made in different segments that fit together.

And yet that's where the similarities seem to end. The EMU looks far more comfortable. It allows free movement and maximum comfort, two things that seem to be sorely lacking in the stormtrooper suit! The EMU also has a Maximum Absorption Garment (MAG), which collects fluids when nature calls. Perhaps the lack of a MAG in the stormtrooper suit explains why stormtroopers are often seen running around urgently!

Buckethead? Are You Receiving Me?

NASA's EMUs cost $12 million apiece. How much would a stormtrooper suit, with all its add-ons and extras, cost in American dollars? A gargantuan cost, that's how much! Here's why: First, the stormtrooper suit had a state-of-the-art combat helmet. It had a comlink, audio pickup, two artificial air-supply hoses, and a broadband comms antenna powered by a single cell. The helmet also had onboard systems for getting breathable air from polluted planets. The helmet also helped the recruit see in darkness, glare, and smoke, though it limited what the recruit could actually see. This may explain why many troopers were such bad marksmen!

A built-in heads-up display also helped stormtroopers shoot their targets (not that you'd notice!), power levels, and environmental readings. A recruit could also access military data and civilian data on the helmet's display. The combat helmet, like a mix of Google Glass and Oculus Rift, sounds like a job as tricky as air traffic control. An average buckethead may not have known whether he was coming, going, or being seduced by the dark side.

With all this going on, maybe Imperial Command knew about the chaos inside the head of a stormtrooper. Imperial Command banned chatter, which was strictly off-limits while on-duty. Stormtrooper helmets recorded all that was said by their users, sending it to Command after downloading from the armor's data banks. Maybe members of Imperial Command spent many a happy hour watching blooper reels of stormtroopers in combat!

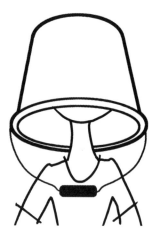

HOW COULD BB-8 HELP US EXPLORE MARS?

It all started with the first trailer for Episode VII. The camera pans over dunes of sweeping sand. Finn suddenly jerks his head into the frame. Then an astromech droid, moving incredibly quickly—with a drive system that is so still compared with the round, rolling body—tears across the sands of Jakku. A rolling ball robot with a floating head! The very sight of this quickly made BB-8 the unofficial droid mascot of *The Force Awakens*. But what if we swap the sands of Jakku for the sands of Mars? How might this orange-and-cream droid help us explore the Red Planet?

Astromech Spec

Astromech droids were a class of repair droid that were used as mechanics on starships. The droids were compact, with most being about one meter tall. They were tooled up through special limbs that were hidden in compartments on the droid body. Many starfighter spacecraft relied on astromech droids to act as copilots. As the droids sat in astromech sockets, exposed to space, they would control flight and power systems, as well as calculating hyperspace jumps and doing routine stuff.

Chatting astromechs were nothing like prattling protocol droids. Astromechs "talked" only through computer systems—that familiar code of clicks, bleeps, and burps. The BB unit was a new class of astromech created sometime after the Battle of Endor, with the main new design being its round body.

What kind of jobs could a BB unit do on Mars? They include: planetary studies for future human exploration, investigating climate and geology, and finding out whether Mars has ever been suitable for life.

Journey to Mars

NASA is on an incredible journey to the Red Planet. The plans include sending humans in the near future. Current and future robotic spacecraft are leading the way and will prepare for those future missions.

One recent robot invention is the use of "relay units." This job seems perfect for BB-8. The relay unit sends radio data from the Martian surface to an orbiter passing overhead. The relay of data from the surface of Mars to orbiters, then from Mars orbit to Earth, helps sample much more data than used to be possible. You just have to remember there's a time lag in data coming from Mars. This can be anything between three and twenty-one minutes, as the distance between Earth and Mars varies from

about 55 million to 378 million kilometers. That's simply because Mars is sometimes on the same side of the sun as us, and sometimes it's not.

A BB unit could also search Mars for radiation harmful to humans, if they were exposed to it. There's an armada of rovers and robots already on and around Mars. They have really helped improve our knowledge of the Red Planet. A BB unit could help pave the way for future human explorers by getting better data about radiation from the Martian surface. The data would help plan how to protect the astronauts when they get there.

Journey to the Center of Mars

Maybe a BB unit's coolest Martian mission would be caving. Earlier in this book we looked at the links between Hoth and Mars. And we talked about NASA's discovery in 2007 of a series of telltale "skylights" in Mars's surface. The skylights meant there may be underground tunnels on Mars, maybe even caverns. The tunnels, made by ancient lava under the Red Planet's surface, may be the secret to understanding Mars's history.

Digging down is the key to discovering Mars's past. Geology works in layers. The more you dig down, the further into the past you delve. It's like the famous story *Journey to the Center of the Earth*, by French sci-fi writer Jules Verne. In the book, a professor gets inside the earth through the cone of an old volcano in Iceland. As the professor delves into the earth, he looks at the rocks, and his journey also becomes a quest into the depths of time.

BB-8 could be sent on a similar mission. The skylights are doorways into Mars. Since geology works in layers, the skylights are like the volcano cone in *Journey to the Center of the Earth*. Inside the skylights there will be hundreds of feet of Martian rock. So, if a unit like BB-8 were to explore the tunnels, the story in the stones could be read without risking human life.

This Martian caving would save huge amounts of time. That's because previous plans for reading Mars's rocks were to be done little by little, layer by layer.

BB-8 Goes Caving

How would BB-8 get into the tunnels?

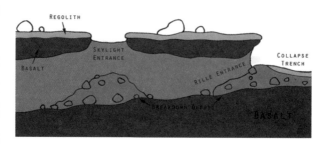

One way would be down through a skylight. But it might be a little tricky. BB-8 would need some kind of repulsorlift tech to stop himself from falling down into the Martian depths. A second option would be drilling, or even blasting, through the roof of the lava tube. BB-8 would need some kind of diamond-tipped drill, hidden away in one of those astromech compartments.

BB-8 should take the easy option. He could simply enter the tunnels through one of the rille entrances. These are like caves into sections of lava tubes. Once inside, BB-8 could begin work. Here in the tunnels are possible future habitats, which are more shielded from the radiation above on Mars's surface. The underground tubes are also better protected

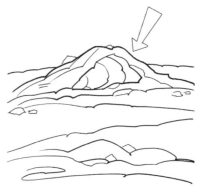

from meteorite impacts and would have more stable temperatures. All this makes the lava tubes good not just for data but also for human living.

Life in the Universe

The caves of Mars may also provide clues about life on the Red Planet. So BB-8 can do some serious science looking for clues that might uncover evidence of life. BB-8 would know that water is the factory of life, giving chemicals the right kind of place to combine and thrive. The elements hydrogen and oxygen make up water. Separate, they are explosive. But together they combine to make the safest of materials, one that doesn't change over a wide range of temperatures. That's why BB-8 would "follow the water" when looking for life on Mars.

But water is not the only essential for life. Life must also be shielded on hostile planets. In the past, Mars had a magnetic field, which protected the planet from harmful rays. BB-8 would be tuned to search for life, which hides deep in the rocks and caves, sheltering from the harsh conditions on the Red Planet.

NASA and other space agencies plan to send humans to Mars. Scientists the world over are working hard to develop the tech that will one day be used to live and work safely on Mars, then return home. We may not yet have BB-8 units to help pave the way. But we know what science needs to be done for the next giant leap into space.

COULD A SINGLE BLAST FROM THE DEATH STAR DESTROY THE EARTH?

How do we answer this question? Well, first up, a Death Star Commander, such as Grand Moff Tarkin, would need to know what kind of wicked weaponry his Death Star actually had on board. According to the stories, the Death Star's main weapon was its super-laser—a weapon powered by "hypermatter." Now, hypermatter isn't really a thing. The word "hyper" is a common sci-fi trick. Sure, it sounds scientific. But it just means "beyond." So "hypermatter" simply means "beyond ordinary matter." Not normal stuff. It's exotic stuff that science hasn't yet discovered. In short, the writers simply don't know!

And yet the Death Star has become the most famous superweapon in science fiction. It has enough firepower to destroy an entire planet! What kind of energies would the Death Star need to annihilate Alderaan, or to vaporize planet Earth? Well, that depends on something called the "binding energy" of the planet. What's binding energy? It's the energy you need to put into a planet for it to stop being held together by gravity. In other words, the energy needed to smash it into smithereens!

Earth and Alderaan seem like very similar planets. So the binding energy the Death Star would need to destroy Earth or Alderaan would be about the same. Alderaan is said to be an earthlike world. It's also 5 billion years old. It's also covered with snowcapped mountains and green pastures. And from space it also looks like a blue-green ball, covered in a web of white clouds. Yep, sounds pretty earthlike!

What's It Take to Destroy the Earth?

So the binding energy the Death Star would need to destroy Earth would be about the same it needed to make Alderaan go *kaboom*. When we do some complicated math, we find that the energy a Death Star Commander would need to destroy Alderaan or Earth is 224,000, 000,000,000,000,000,000,000,000 joules of energy. That's a pretty impressive bundle of energy.

Let's get some kind of ballpark feeling for how much energy this is. (You will have to check out some of the number-words in this paragraph on Google!) The bundle of energy is 200 sextillion times the energy in an average lightning bolt. Or 20 quadrillion times the energy released by a severe thunderstorm. Or roughly half a billion times the amount of energy that was released when that famous asteroid crashed into the earth and killed off the dinosaurs.

Another way of looking at it is this. The total energy output of our sun, each second, is 380,000,000,000,000,000,000,000,000 joules. That means the sun would make the energy the Death Star needed to destroy the earth in 6.8 days. So, a week's worth of sunshine could destroy the earth. But how does the Death Star conjure up that amount of energy to do the job?

What About an Antimatter Bomb?

Antimatter might do it. The Death Star super-laser could deliver an antimatter bomb. The Death Star weapon could guide a huge antimatter bomb into the heart of a planet like the earth. Now, antimatter does not easily exist in our universe—only trillionths of a gram have been made in real laboratories. The Death Star would need tons of the stuff.

But the potential energy of antimatter is truly huge. When antimatter joins explosively with ordinary matter, the result is 100 percent mutual destruction. Einstein's famous equation $E=mc^2$ applies here. It means a small amount of mass (that's the "m" in Einstein's equation) is converted into a huge amount of energy (the "E" in Einstein's equation). For example, an amount of antimatter the same mass as a car could produce all of the world's electricity for one year!

So exactly how much antimatter would a Death Star commander need to get his hands on? Around one and a quarter trillion tons of the stuff! This antimatter bomb would be about 20,000 times less massive than the asteroid 16 Psyche, which we mentioned in our calculation of the cost of building the Death Star. One and a quarter trillion tons of antimatter would make a sphere three kilometers across, about sixty times smaller than our asteroid.

This is a huge bomb. But with a diameter of 120 kilometers, the Death Star could easily house it. In fact, think about the super-laser cannon well—that's the huge dimple in the surface of the Death Star. The central hole of that cannon well is around 6 kilometers across, easily wide enough from which to project our antimatter bomb.

Now think about the Death Star's tractor beams. They could be used to make a force field that can push or pull an antimatter bomb. In *Star Wars*, such devices were often found on vessels, creating an energy field that allowed them to lock on to, and move, other vessels or objects. "Wait, hang on," you might be saying. "Wouldn't the bomb burn up as it passed through the Earth's atmosphere?" After all, when antimatter meets ordinary matter, the result is *kaboom*.

But there's a cunning solution that the crafty Commander may consider! The Death Star could make antimatter bullets. Let's say these bullets are made of anti-Lucasonium, named after *Star Wars* movie director George Lucas. Anti-Lucasonium is a super-dense material with a billion kilograms for every cubic centimeter. This would be fired into the earth's core. But the anti-Lucasonium bullet isn't destroyed. Instead, as it plunges down to the earth's core, it acquires a protective coat of plasma. Next a regular bullet of Lucasonium is fired in. This also falls to the core, at a time cleverly calculated to meet the first bullet head-on, at the very core of the earth. At this instant, the two bullets destroy each other and the earth at the same time. Not only is this option very efficient, but it also has the advantage of releasing all the energy at the earth's core, doing most damage.

Such Death Star antimatter bombs wouldn't be the earth's first extinction event. But it would certainly be its last.

WILL OUR FUTURE MEGACITIES LOOK LIKE THE CITIES OF CORUSCANT?

n *Star Wars*, Coruscant was a city that covered an entire planet. The top-level skyscrapers of Coruscant were the homes and businesses for the rich and powerful. The elites were ferried through the buzzing sky-lanes by air-speeders, which wove from one tower to the next. Traffic was constant. But crashes were rare, as speeders came with navigational systems that made them run along preprogrammed paths.

Among the elite were the Supreme Chancellor and members of the Galactic Senate. These rich and powerful people thrived in lavish lifestyles. They lounged in high-rise penthouses. They dined in fine restaurants. Even when the Republic began to die, and the Clone Wars raged on, the elite carried on in their usual way, breathing air that was clean and filtered.

Sunlight never reached the lower levels. The Coruscant underworld was a different story. As Sheev Palpatine once said to Anakin, "Do you know the rarest resource on Coruscant, my boy? Sky. Down here, the sun is a myth." It's a long way down from the highest level on Coruscant, Level 5127, to the lowest, Level 1. The underworld had to be lit by artificial light. And its people were forced to breathe poisonous air from factory and vehicle pollution. The underworld was where Coruscant's criminal class lived. The underworld was a huge city beneath the city. The many millions who were too poor to move upward lived in the bowels of the city. Such citizens rarely, if ever, saw the surface of the planet during their lifetimes.

Future Cities on Earth

How does Coruscant compare with future visions of Earth cities? At the moment, it seems humans are unsure about what a city will look like in the future. But it's clear that the future will only contain what we put into it now. So, rather than a sudden leap into dazzling *Star Wars*–style cityscapes, planners and architects need to respond to what Earth cities might face in the future.

So, one of the things future cities must have is survivability—an ability to actually survive changes. Our civilization relies on just the one planet. The *Star Wars* galaxy had other options. *Star Wars* planets could ship in stuff from "summer planets," where mostly farming was done. Earth is all we have at the moment.

Three quarters of our planet's major cities lie on the coasts. Take China, the coming superpower of the twenty-first century. Each year, 20 million people migrate to Chinese cities, with the flood-prone Pearl River Delta now the world's largest city area. Worldwide, over a billion people in coastal cities will be vulnerable to serious flooding and extreme weather due to climate change by 2070. Millions more face knock-on effects, such as freshwater shortages and refugees.

Water Is the Watchword

The smart city of the future may be the floating city. Because of climate change and rising seawaters, the future-city planners may take the defensive approach. And that means building cities that keep the water at bay. But in the face of the flowing tide, defense is not the only option. The city could be raised above the water.

Future cities could simply change according to a rising sea level. The levels of Coruscant were many. The future cities of Earth could be designed to simply allow the water in and then adapt. The border between city and sea will change with time, and hopefully win the human battle with the elements.

In the making of *The Force Awakens*, *Star Wars* producers first considered the idea of Jakku as a water planet. Earth already is one. So, if you want a future vision of a terrestrial city, think less like Coruscant and more like Venice! Venice is a city with water under its skirts. Flooded subways, tubeways and sidewalks. Transport not by airspeeder, but by boat. A slower and kinder lifestyle, a quieter type of city, without the constant thrum of engines. Rather than battling against nature, the futuristic city on Earth will welcome life on a (mostly!) water planet.

CAN YOU REALLY SURVIVE BEING FROZEN IN CARBONITE?

As Han Solo knows, there's more than one way to crack time travel. First, there's the Einstein way. Professor Einstein showed that if you travel in a spaceship long enough, at speeds close to that of light, you can return to Earth, centuries in the future. Would-be time travelers are still waiting, living their lives second after second, for such a spaceship to be made.

Second, there's the icy way. The method of choice here is not the spaceship, but the fridge. Medicine is now able to switch people off for a period of time, leaving them with no heartbeat or brain activity. The method is used for some surgery, where patients are frozen as if time stopped . . . and restarted an hour later.

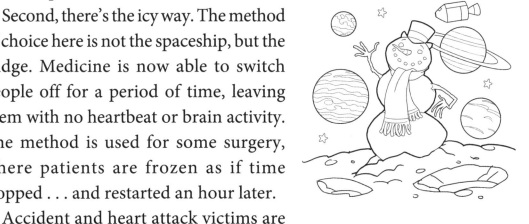

Accident and heart attack victims are brought back from the dead on a daily basis. This is done using CPR (CPR means cardiopulmonary resuscitation—in other words, cranking up your heart). Patients' bodies are often cooled by neurosurgeons, so they can operate on the brain without harm. Babies are born from a mother whose eggs are frozen in fertility clinics, defrosted, and safely implanted.

Cryonics

The icy way is based on cryonics. Cryonics is the idea of storing humans in very cold temperatures, with the hope of defrosting them sometime in the future. The idea is that, if someone has "died" from a disease that is incurable today, it may not be incurable in the future. So the patient can be "frozen" and then brought back in the future when a cure has been uncovered. A person saved this way is said to be in "cryonic suspension."

If you wonder about the ideas behind cryonics, think of the news stories about people who've fallen into a frozen lake and been stuck for up to an hour in the icy water before being rescued. Those who survived did so because the freezing water put their body into a sort of suspension. Their body and brain functions were slowed down so much that they needed almost no oxygen.

Of course, this is what happens to Han Solo, too. During the Galactic Civil War, Darth Vader blackmails Lando Calrissian into letting him use a carbon-freezing device on Han. Solo survives the ordeal, but it could have ended up a lot worse.

Carbonite

So, what exactly is carbonite? According to the *Star Wars* stories, carbonite was a liquid, made from carbon, which could change into a solid through rapid freezing. Firstly, carbon is an excellent choice. We've written in this book (see page 71) about how varied carbon is.

It can bond with life's other main elements to form the backbone of biology. And it also forms most of the chemicals known to humans.

The *Star Wars* description of carbonite says that it was used before the invention of the hyperdrive, with early spacers (a slang term for someone who spent a large part of their life in space) using carbonite to last the long journeys. But carbonite had bad side effects, known as hibernation sickness. So no wonder that bounty hunter Boba Fett was worried Han Solo would be iced for good when covered in carbonite.

Don't Try This at Home

Turns out Boba Fett had good reason for concern. On Earth, of course, it's illegal to perform cryonic suspension on someone who is still alive. So please don't try it at home. Research shows that freezing damages your tissues, so that stuff leaks out of you when your temperature is raised again. Try this at home: freeze and defrost a strawberry and you will soon have a good idea of the mushy mess that Han might become!

So, even though a person may look okay on the surface, underneath, the damage is disastrous. And yet there are some creatures in nature that can survive the freezing process—some frogs, fish, turtles, and insects. Their bodies make huge amounts of the sugar glucose, a natural antifreeze that prevents ice crystals forming. Sadly, there's not enough glucose in humans to do the same, so humans would get frozen with a side effect of death.

Let's look at how "freezing" people on Earth might show us some secrets about what might have happened to Han. When folk are taken to a cryonics clinic, they aren't simply slammed into a vat of liquid nitrogen.

The water inside their cells would freeze. When water freezes, it expands. Their cells would simply shatter. So, instead, the cryonics experts must somehow remove water from the cells and swap it with a sort of human antifreeze. This antifreeze is trying to make humans a bit like frogs and fishes. They have a natural antifreeze that protects their organs and tissues from ice crystals forming at low temperatures. And it puts the cells into a kind of suspended animation.

Now comes the tricky bit. Once water is replaced with antifreeze, the human body is cooled on a bed of dry ice until it reaches –130°C (–202°F). Next, the body is placed in a container, which is put in a large metal tank filled with liquid nitrogen at a cool –196°C (–320°F). The body is stored head down, and for good reason. If there were ever a leak in the tank, the brain would still be in the freezing liquid. Unlike Han, earthlings in cryonic suspension have yet to be revived with success. But some people predict that the first cryonic revival might occur around the year 2040.

Your Local 24/7 Cryonics Store

If you should meet your demise while reading this book (granted, that's unlikely), you could always try cryonics out for yourself, of course. Try, by choice, something that Han Solo had no choice in trying.

Cryonics is big business, but it isn't cheap. It can cost up to $150,000 to have a whole body done. For those with less money, you can preserve just your brain for a cool $50,000. Keep your fingers crossed that, should you go for this brain option, technology will someday come up with a way to clone the rest of you!

Cryonics scientists are working on chemicals that carry out the carbon-freezing function with less death. Maybe Han Solo was pumped full of these. The good news is, once the freezing process is done, a study recently done showed that memories are preserved, at least in worms.

ALSO AVAILABLE

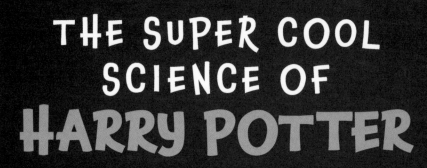

THE SUPER COOL SCIENCE OF HARRY POTTER

The Spell-Binding Science Behind the Magic, Creatures, Witches, and Wizards of the Potter Universe!

AN UNOFFICIAL GUIDE

MARK BRAKE

coauthor of *The Science of Harry Potter* and author of *The Super Cool Science of Star Wars*